I0463655

Robert Jiménez
P.O. Box 260491
Pembroke Pines, FL 33026

www.zerostreet.com
www.tikitower.com
www.strangewise.com

ISBN-13: 978-1543208788
ISBN-10: 1543208789

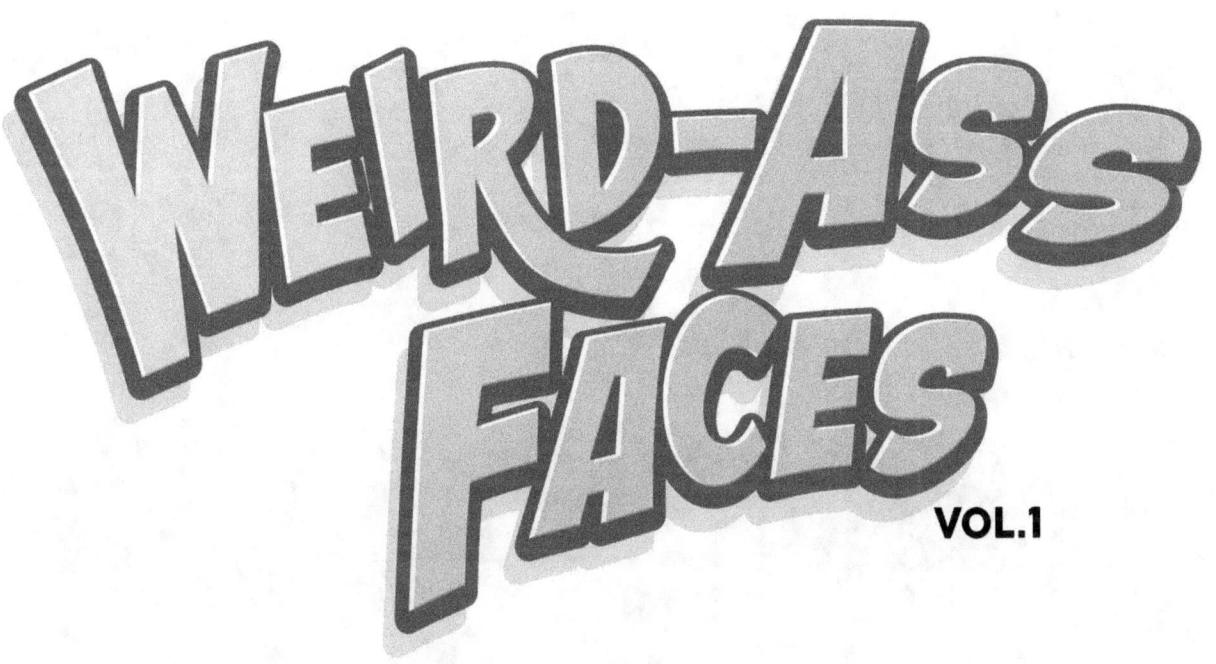

Color 'em Up Pretty!

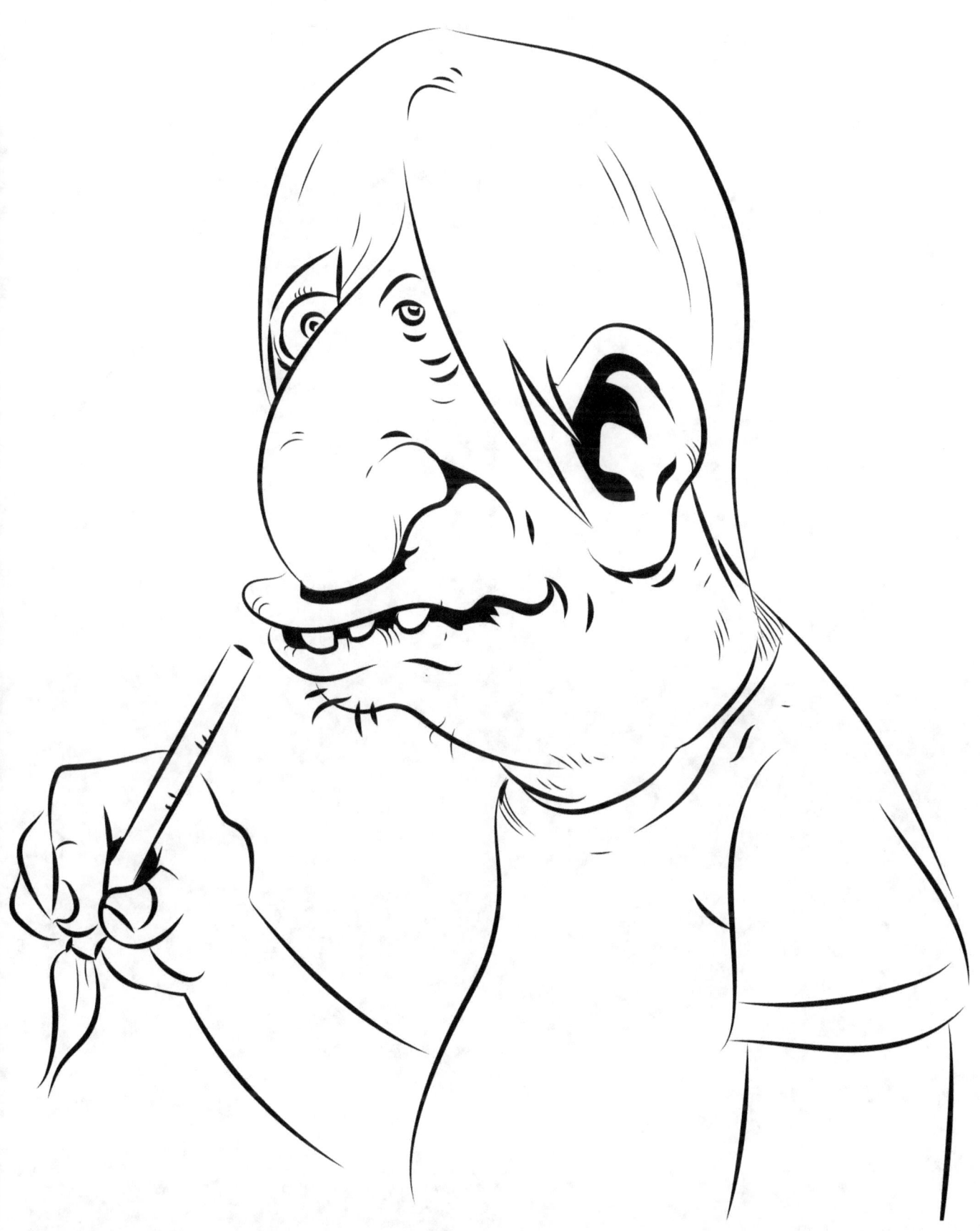

THE IMAGES IN THIS BOOK ARE PRINTED SINGLE-SIDED SO AS TO PREVENT COLORS BLEEDING THROUGH. HOWEVER, WE STILL RECOMMEND USING A SHEET OF PAPER IN BETWEEN PAGES WHILE COLORING, ESPECIALLY WHEN USING MARKERS!

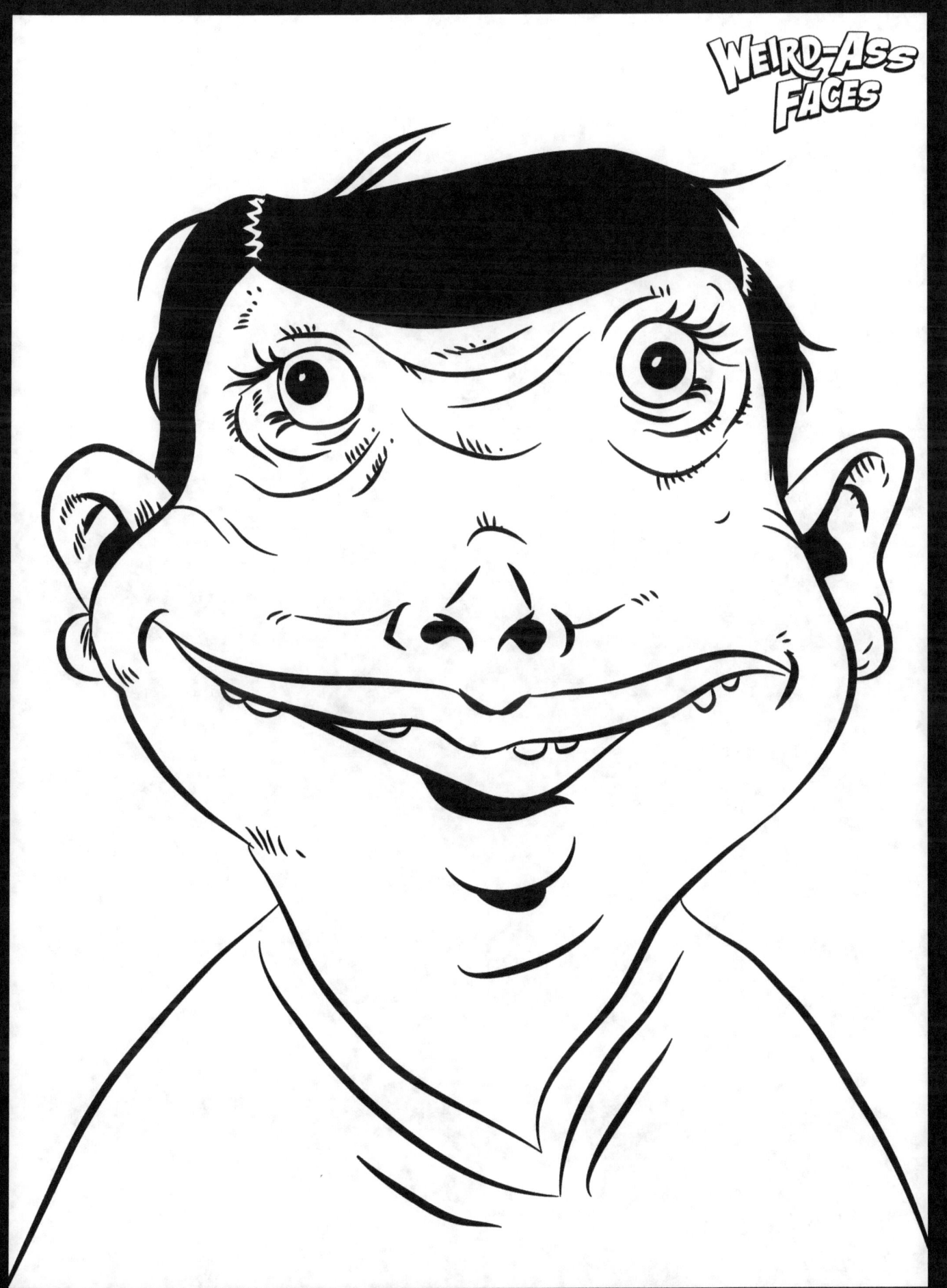

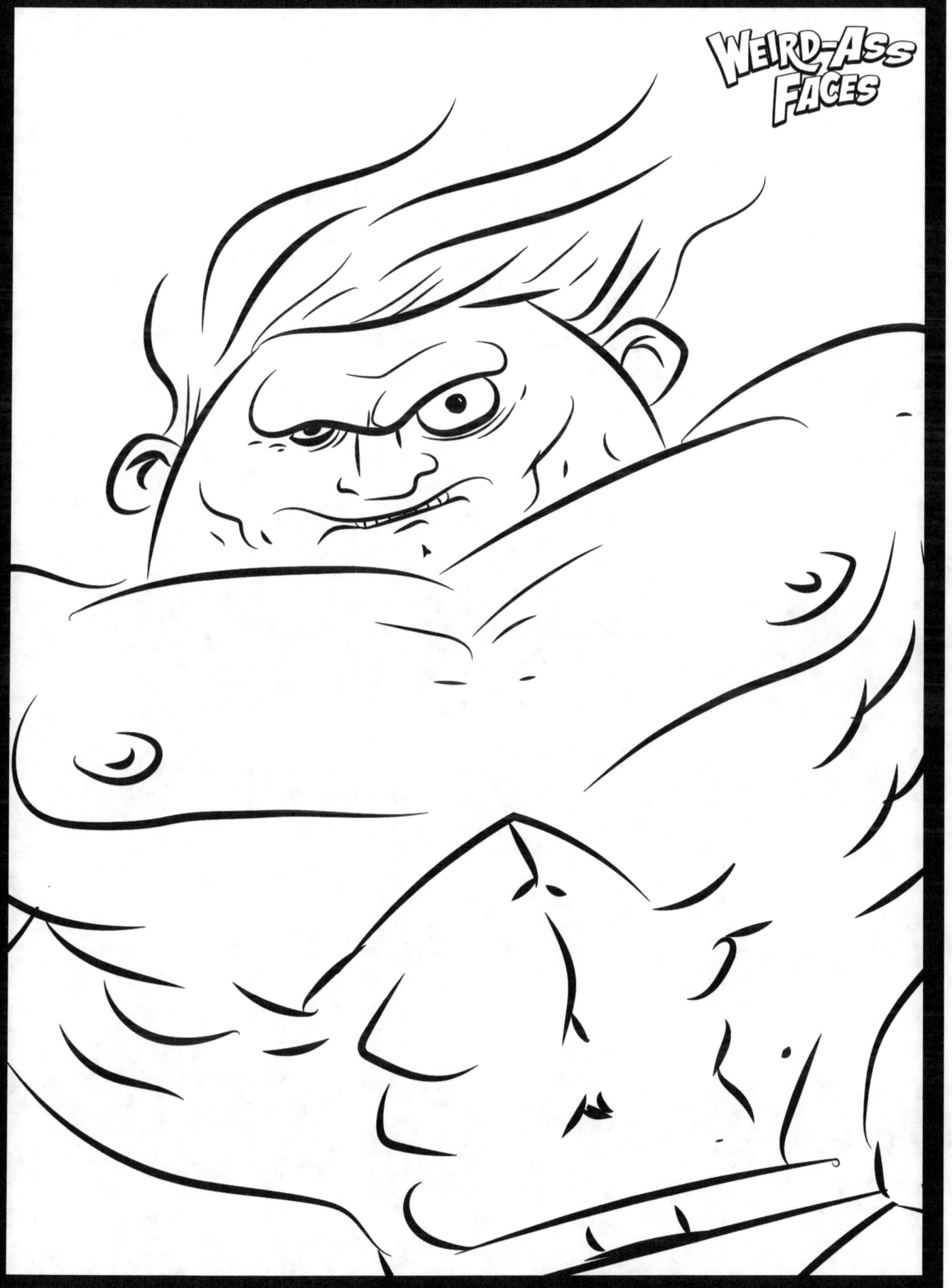

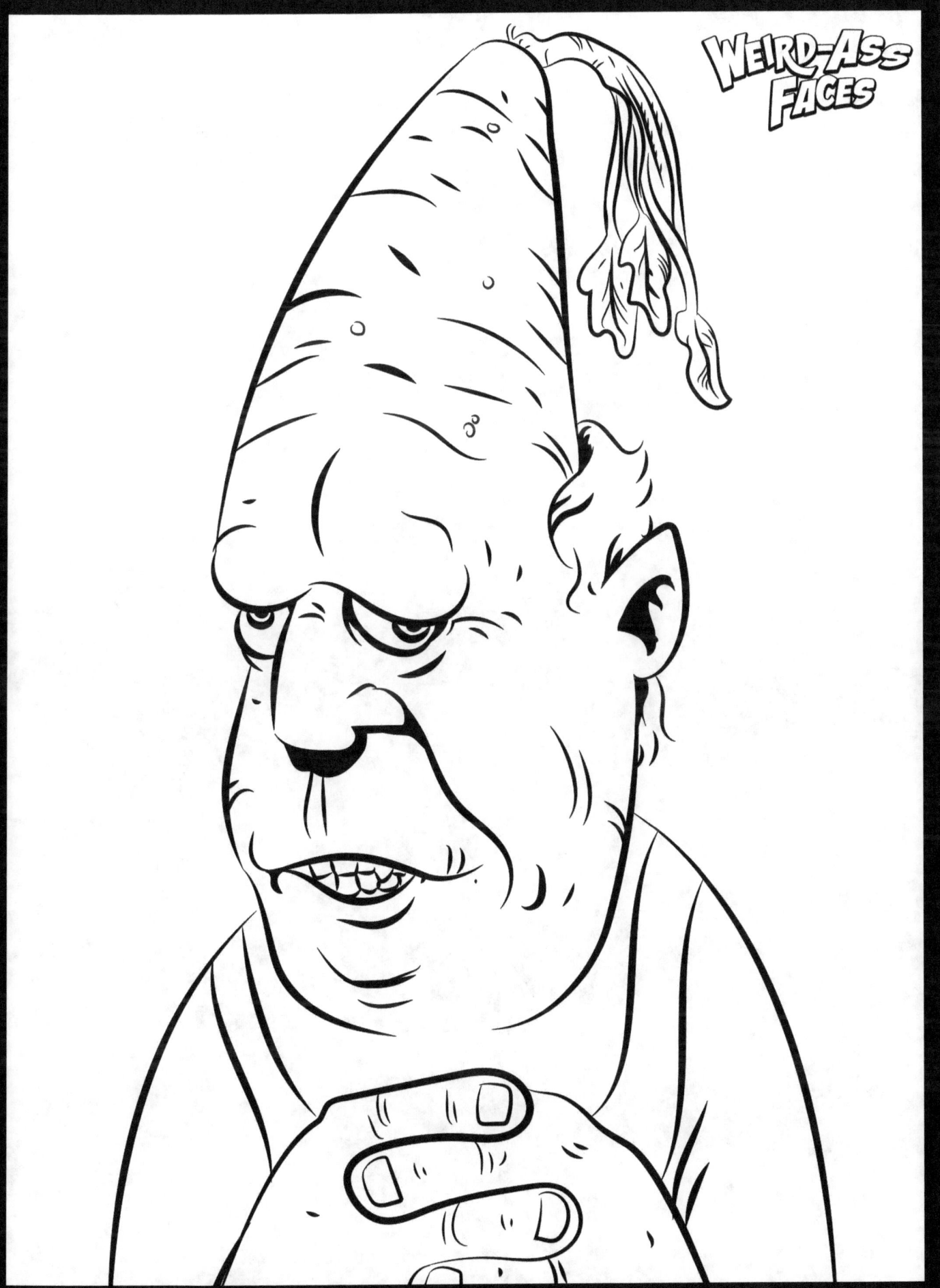

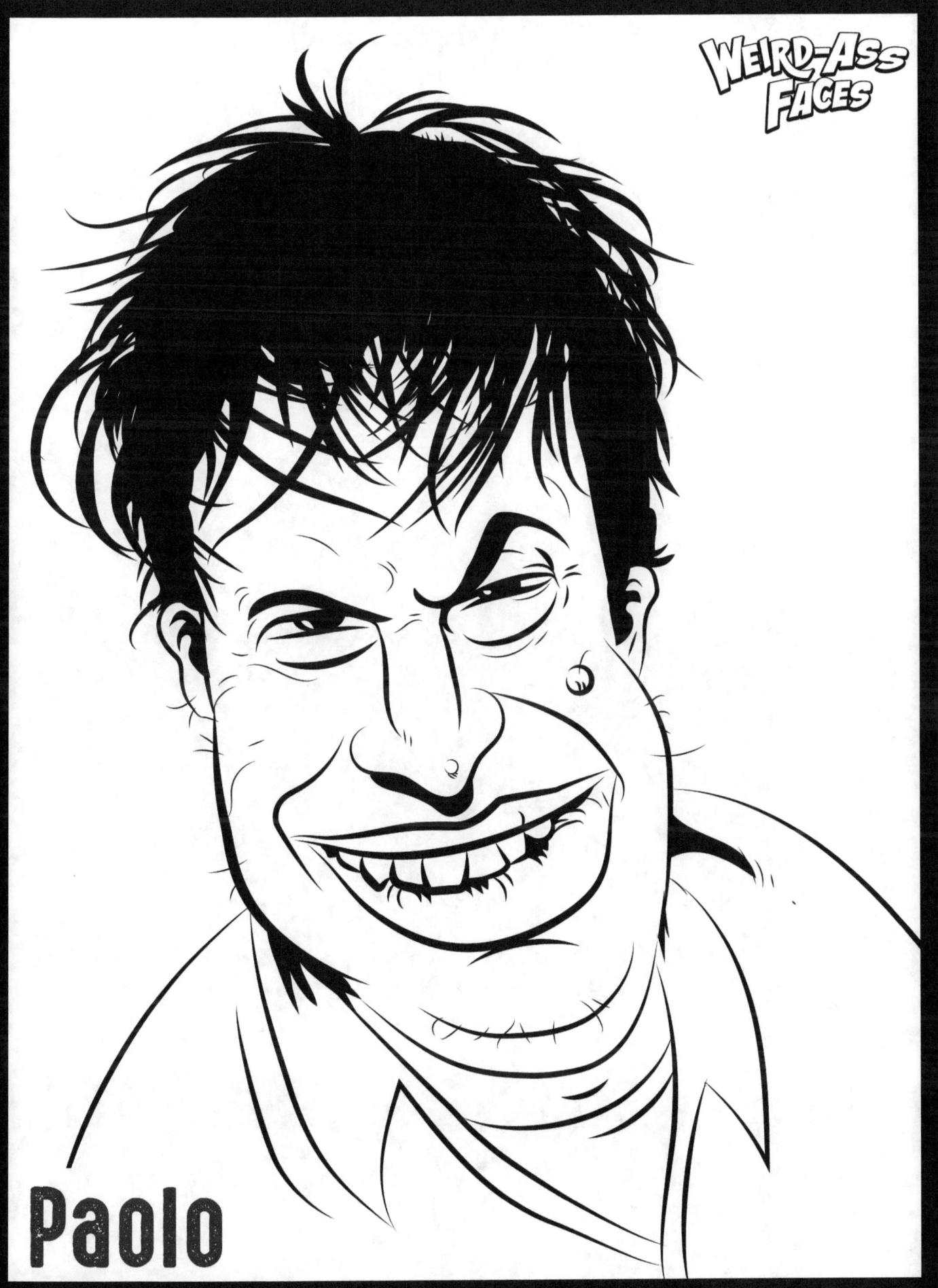

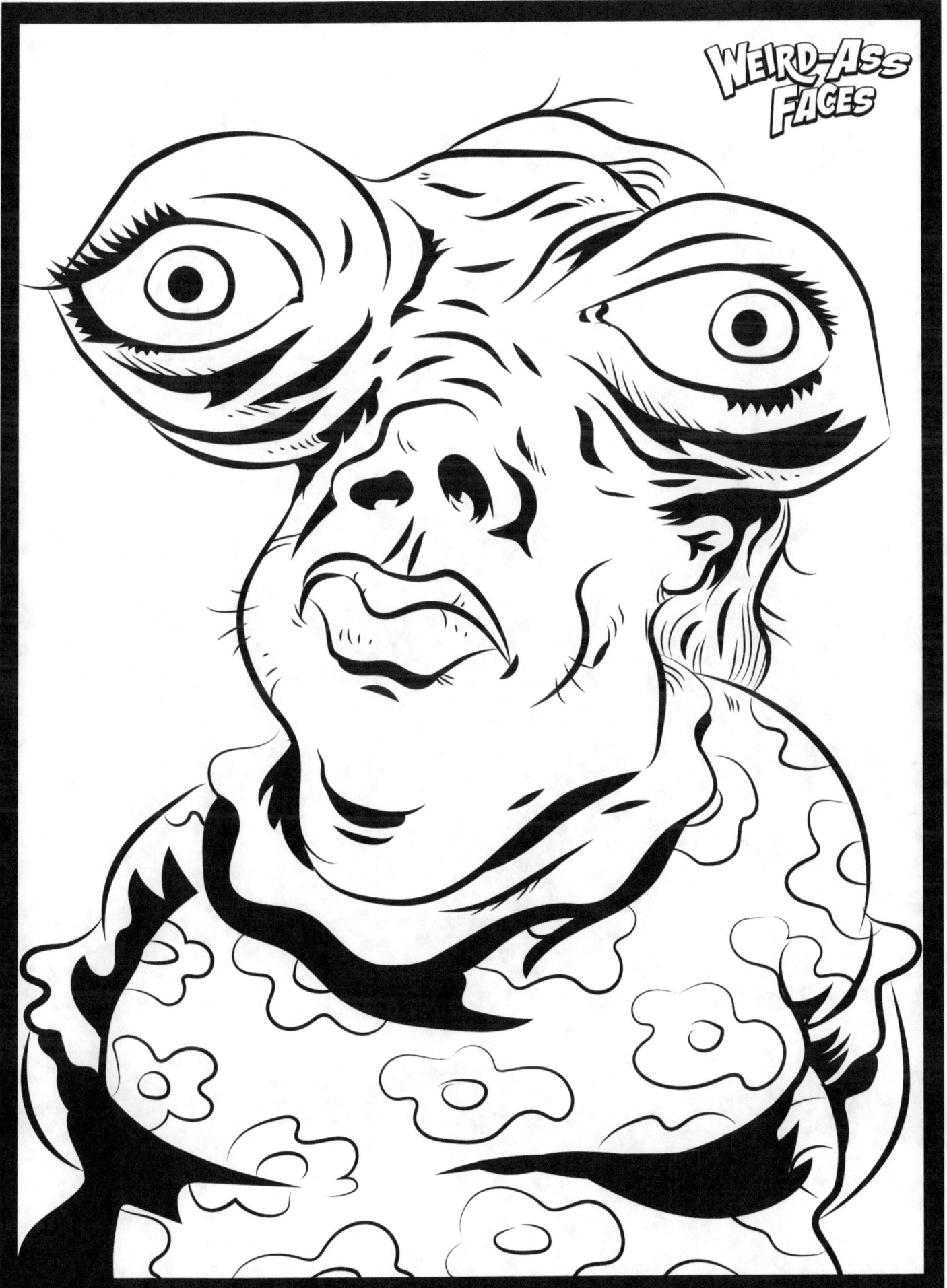

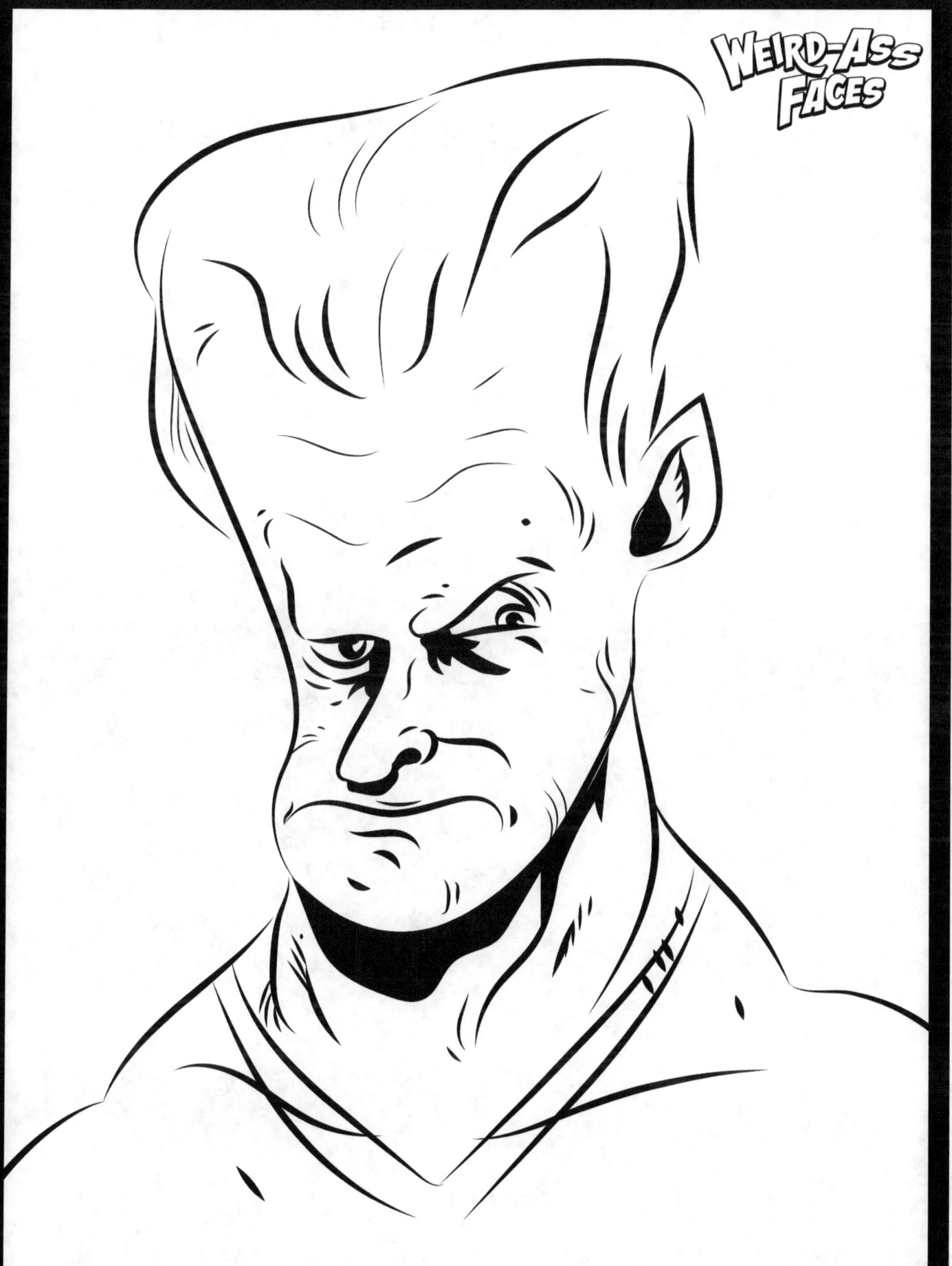

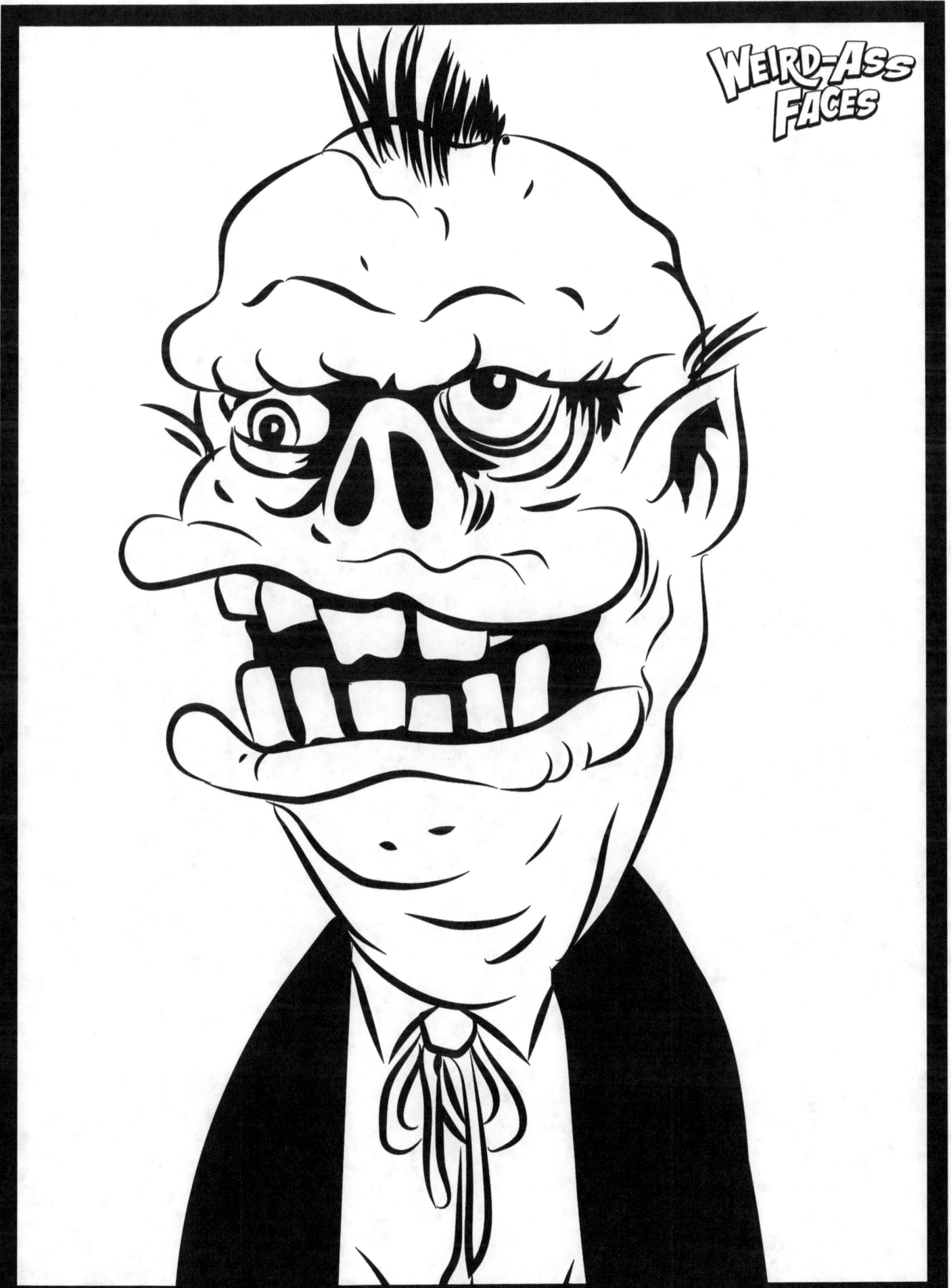

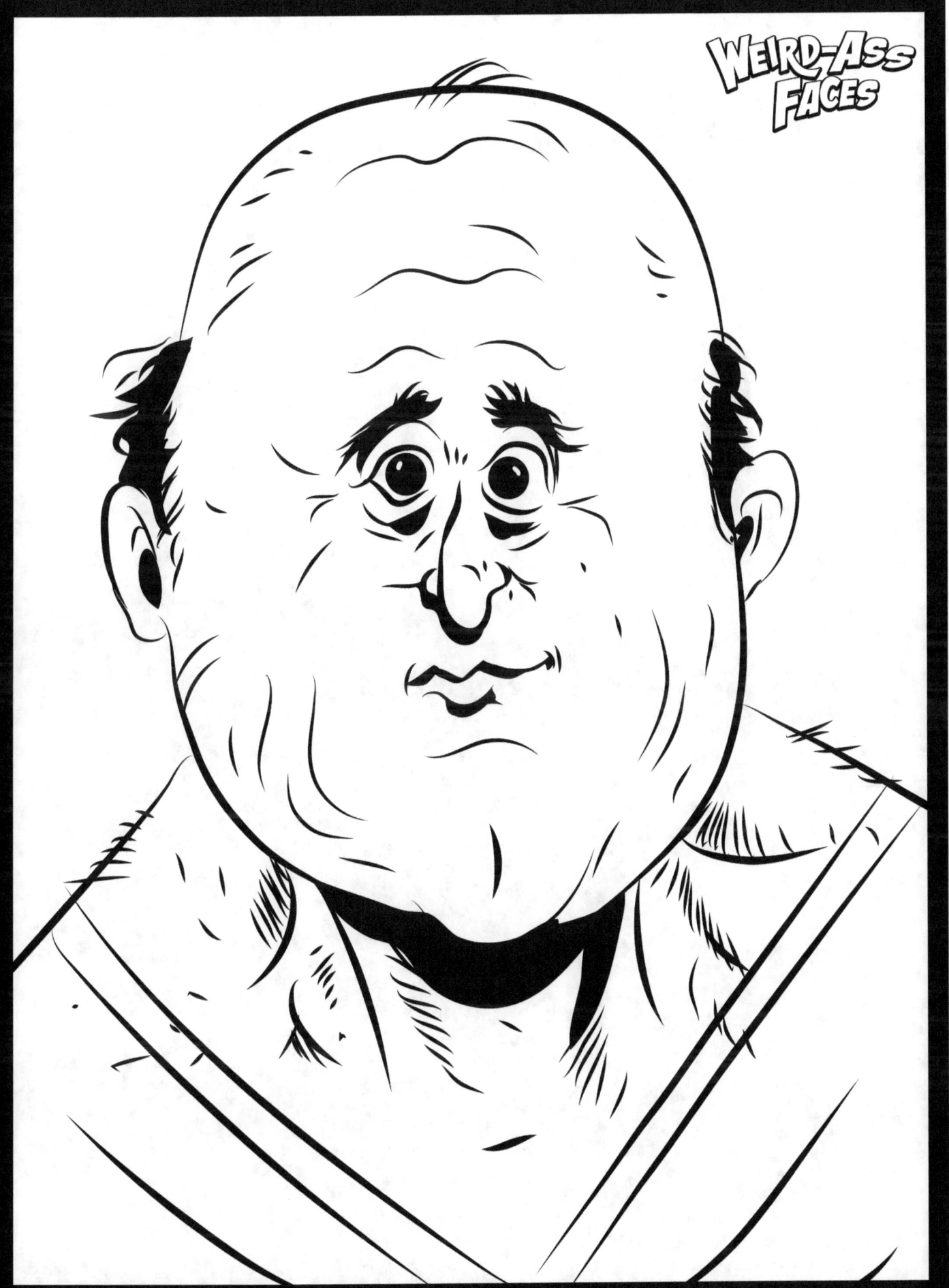

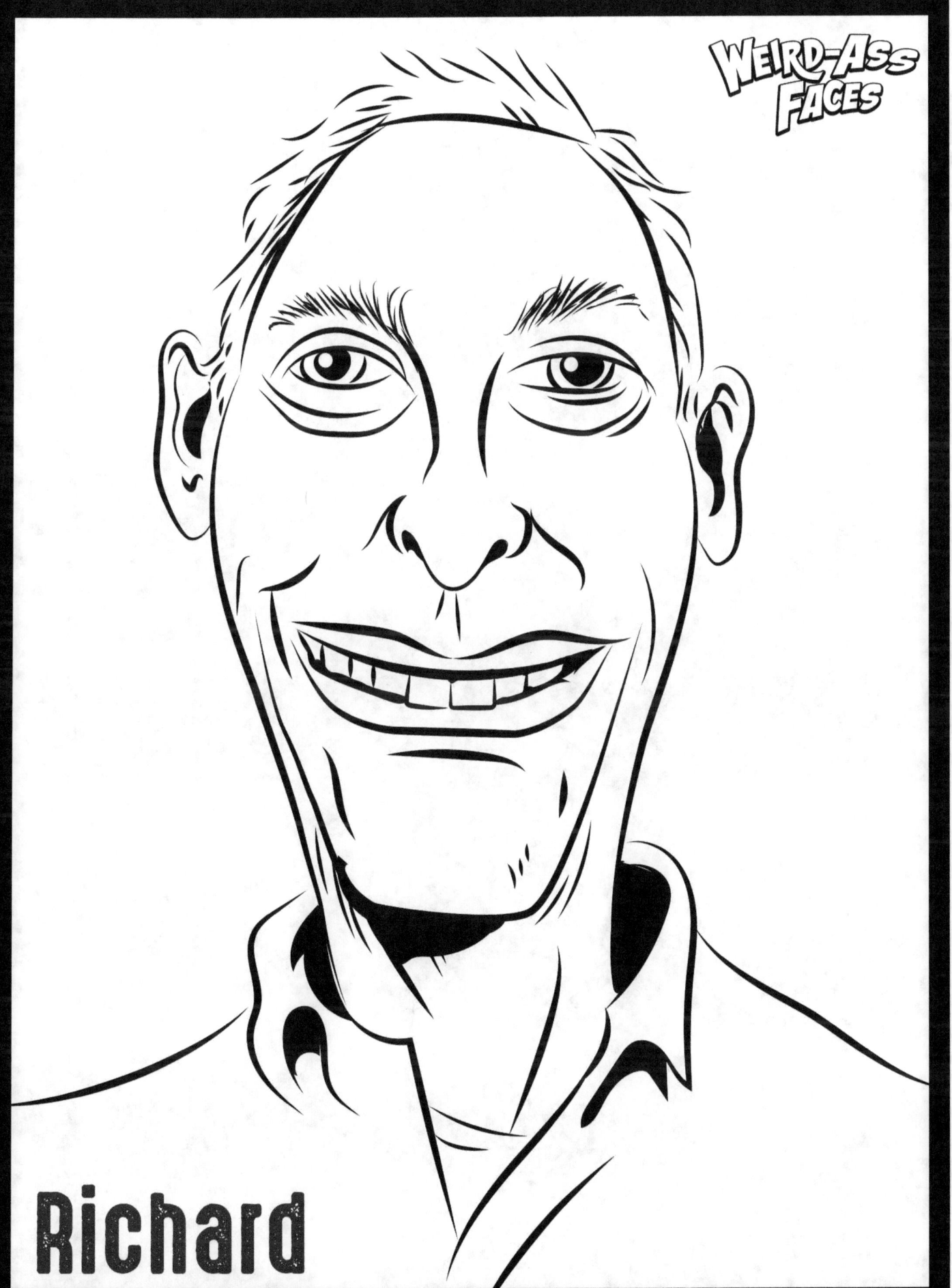

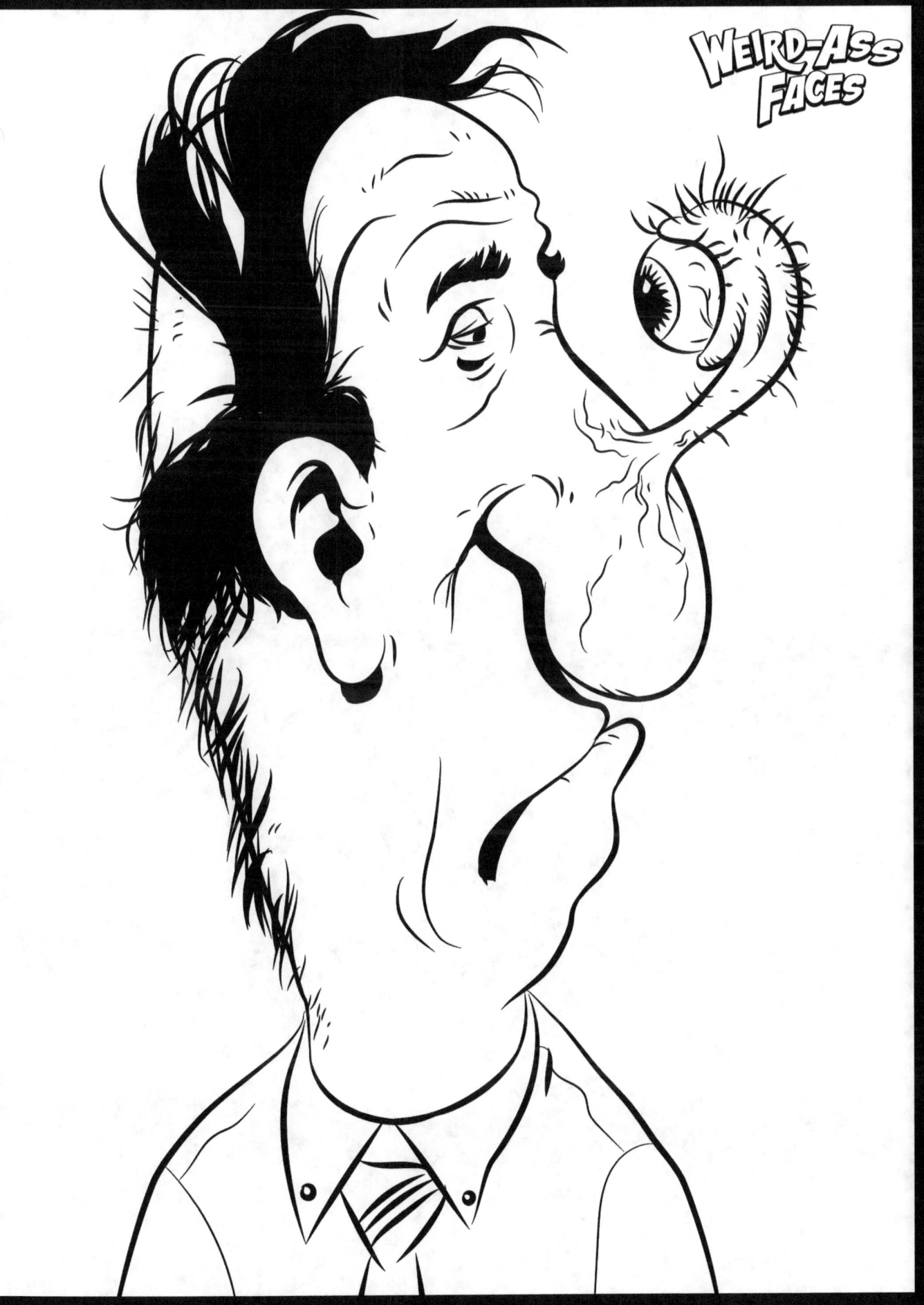

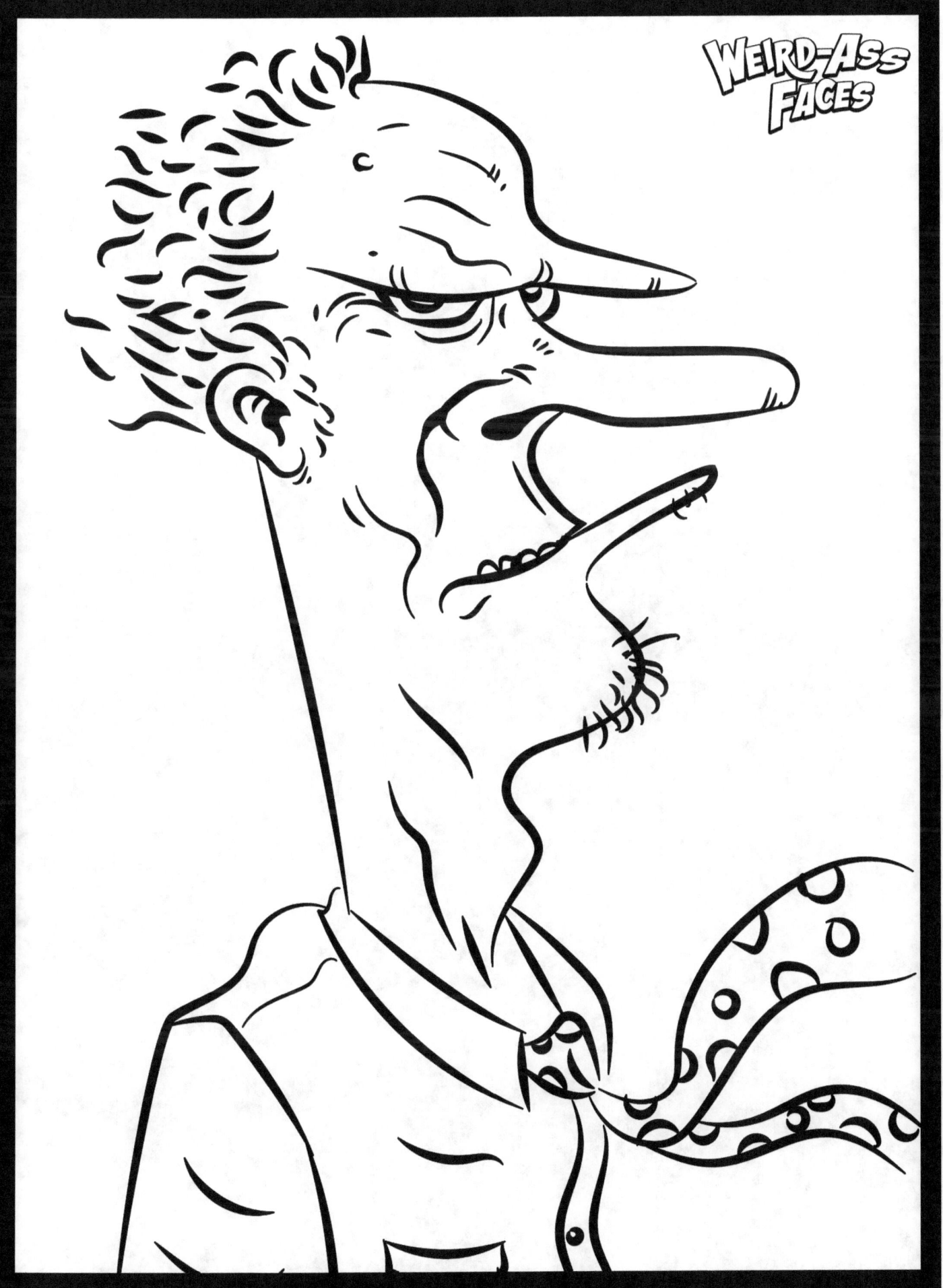

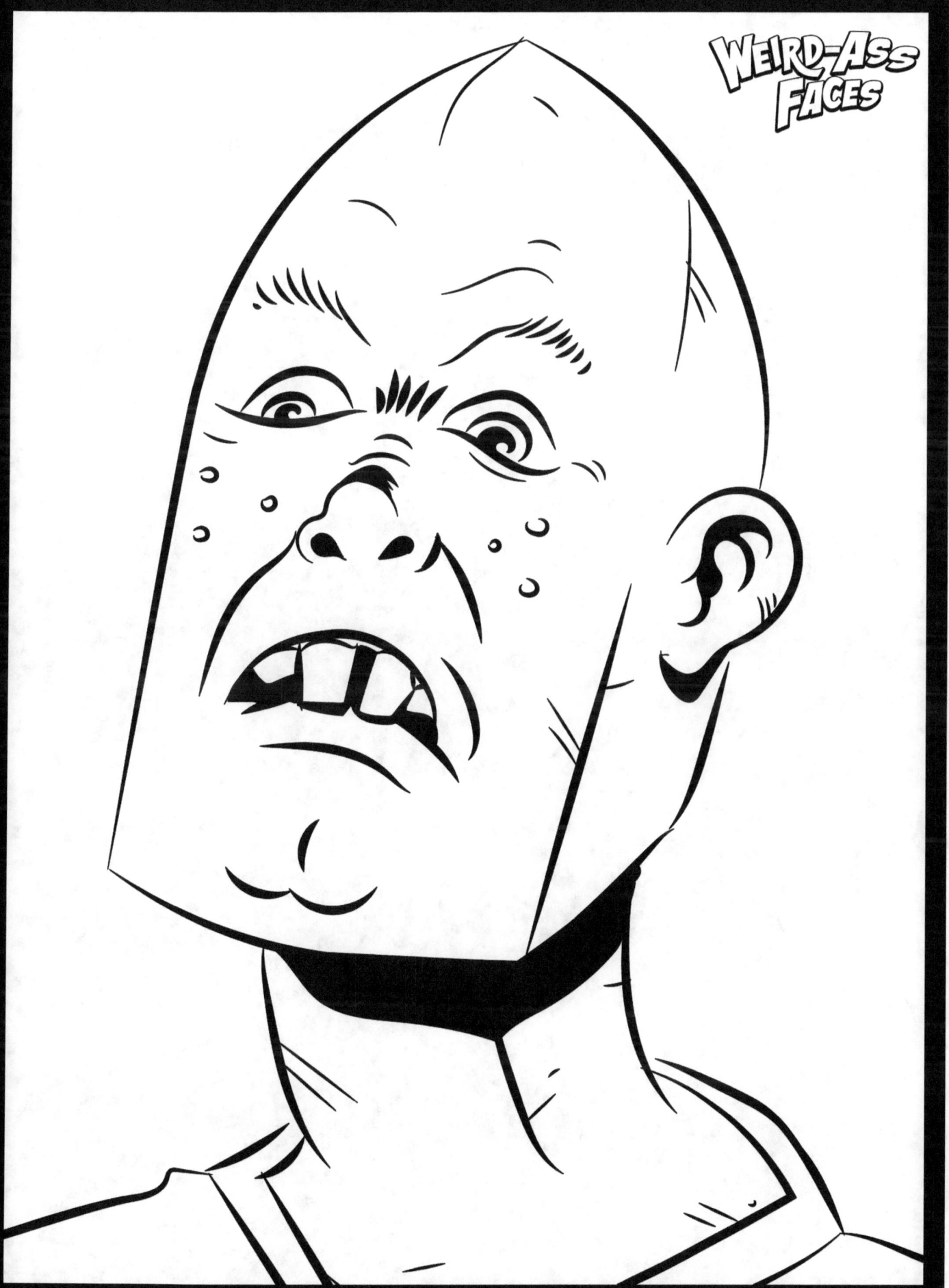

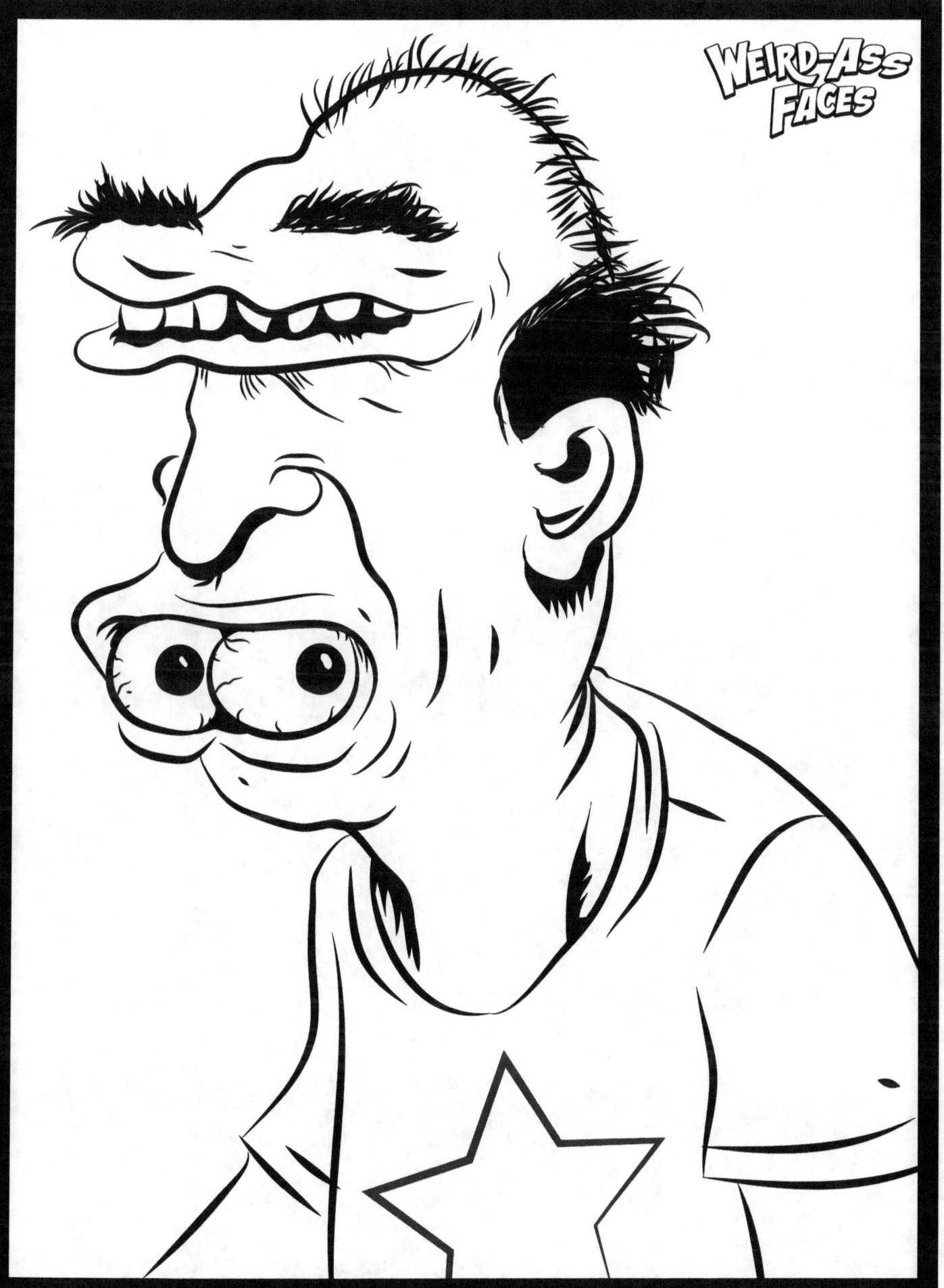

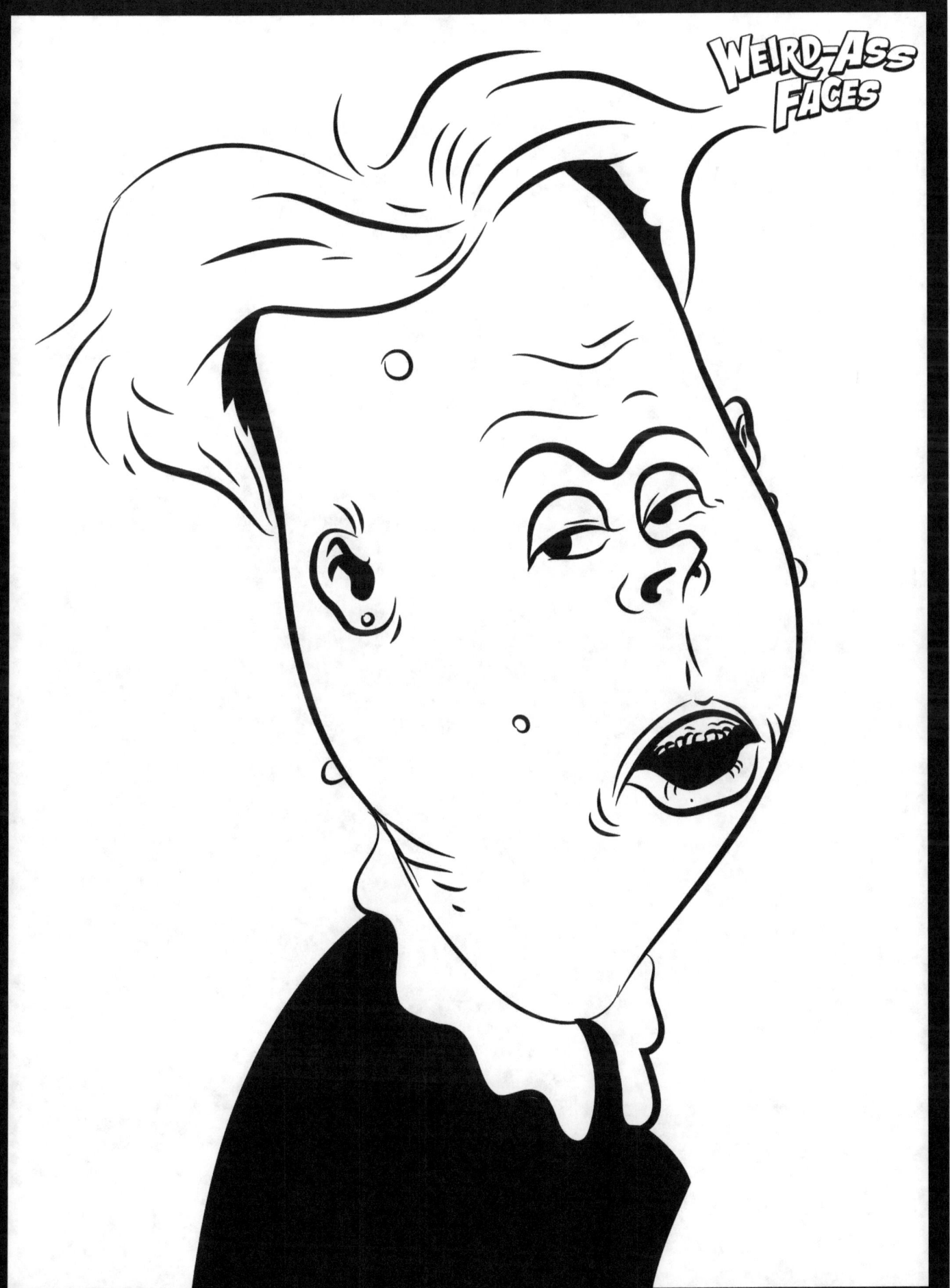

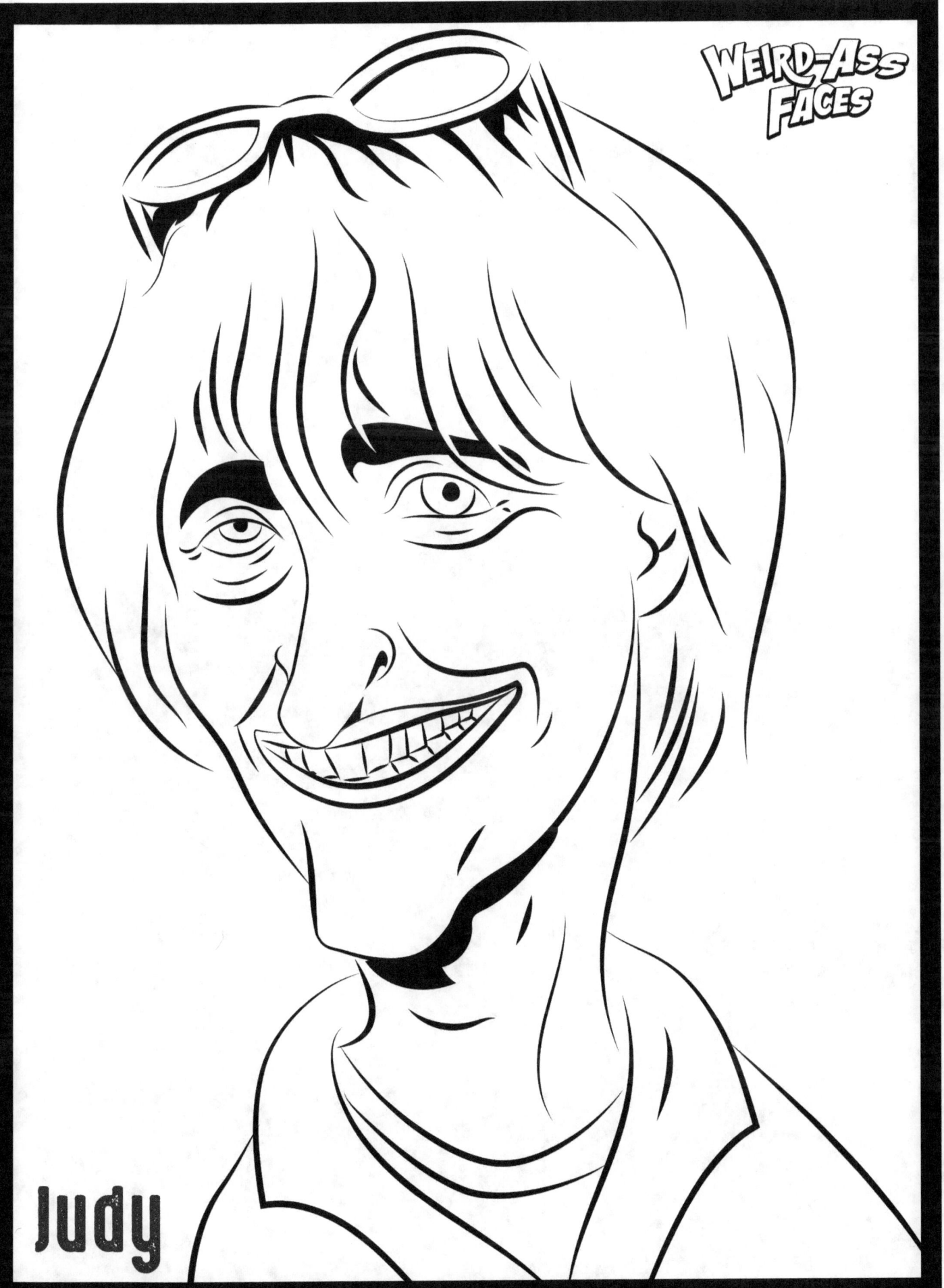

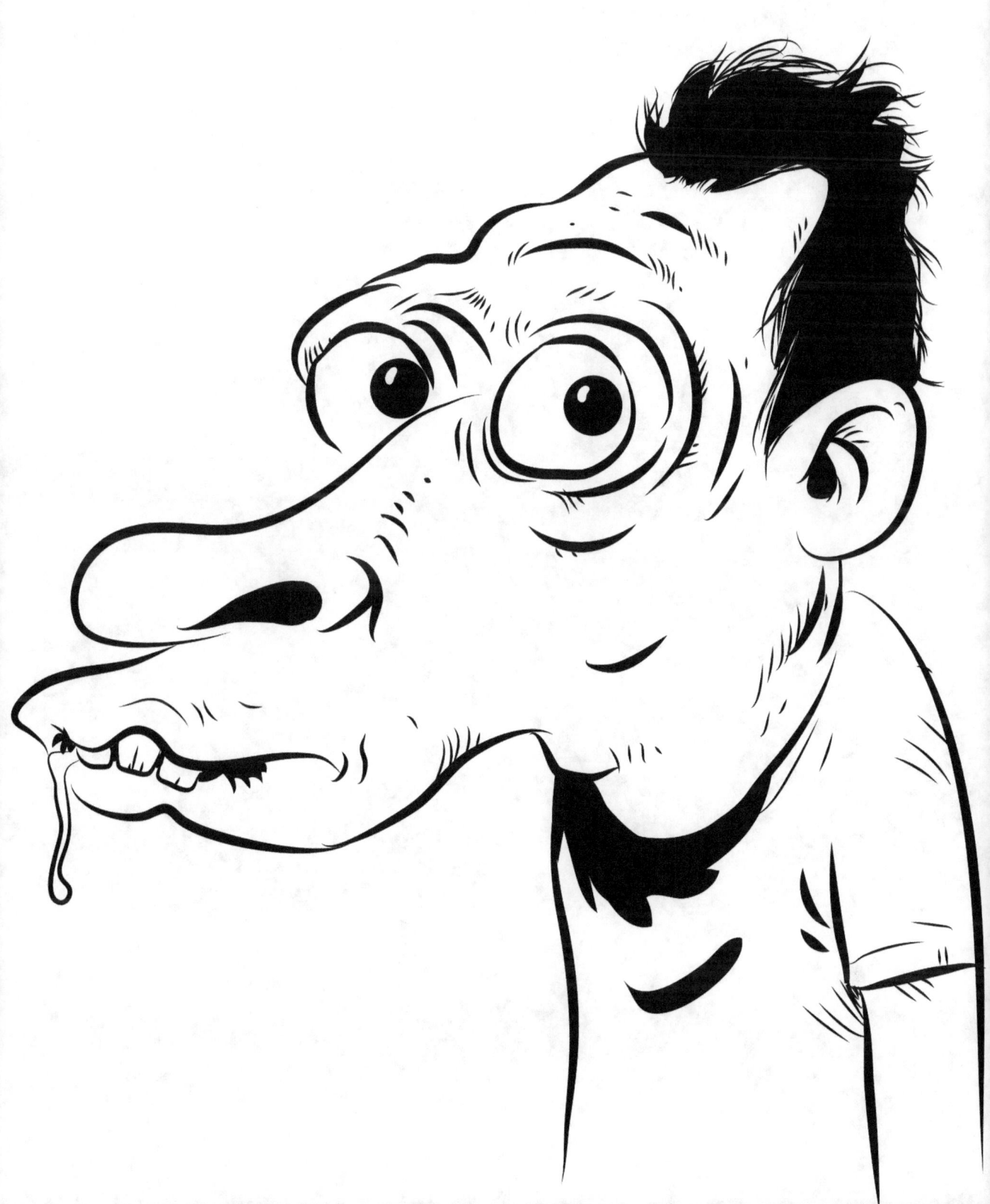

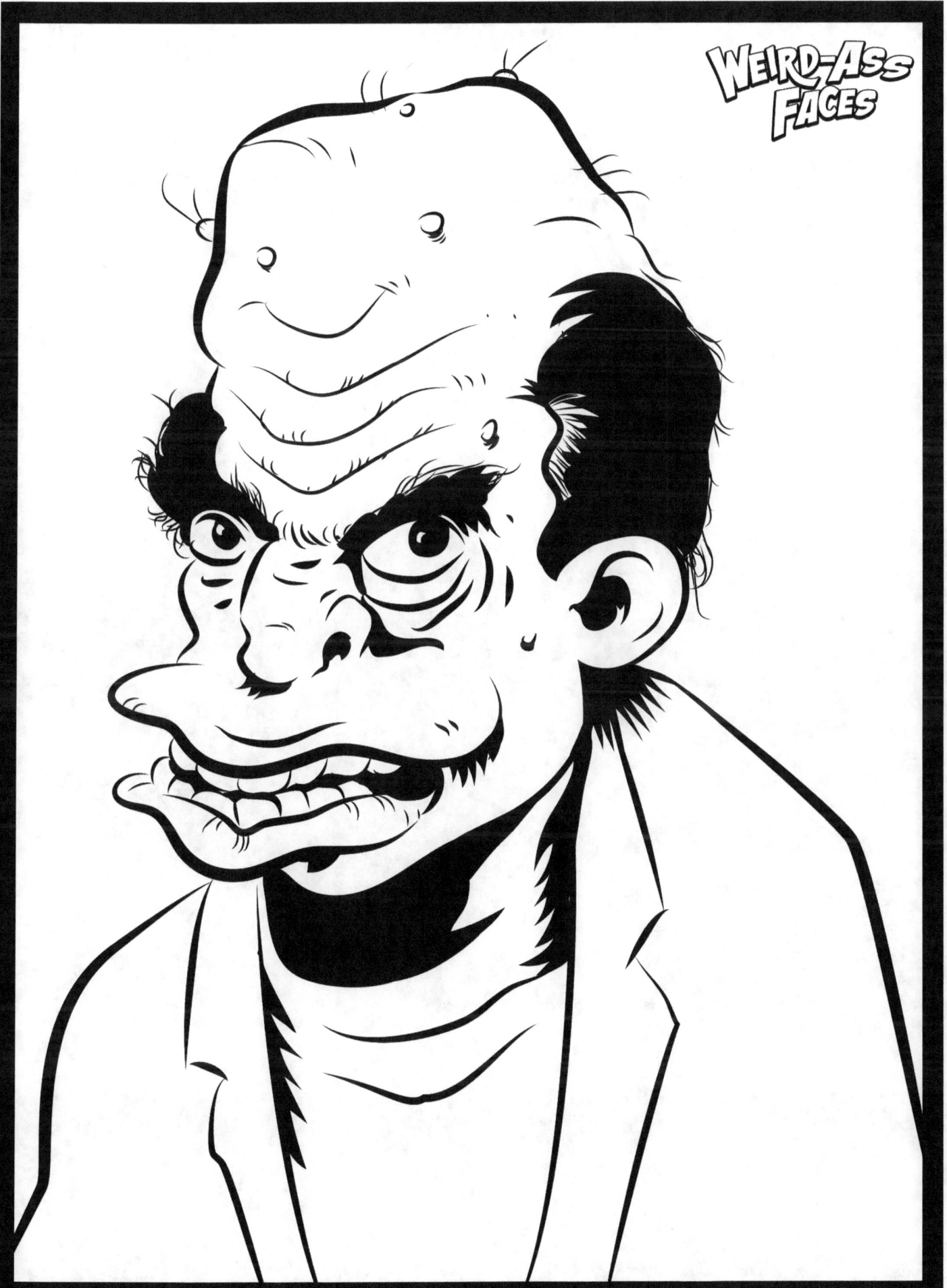

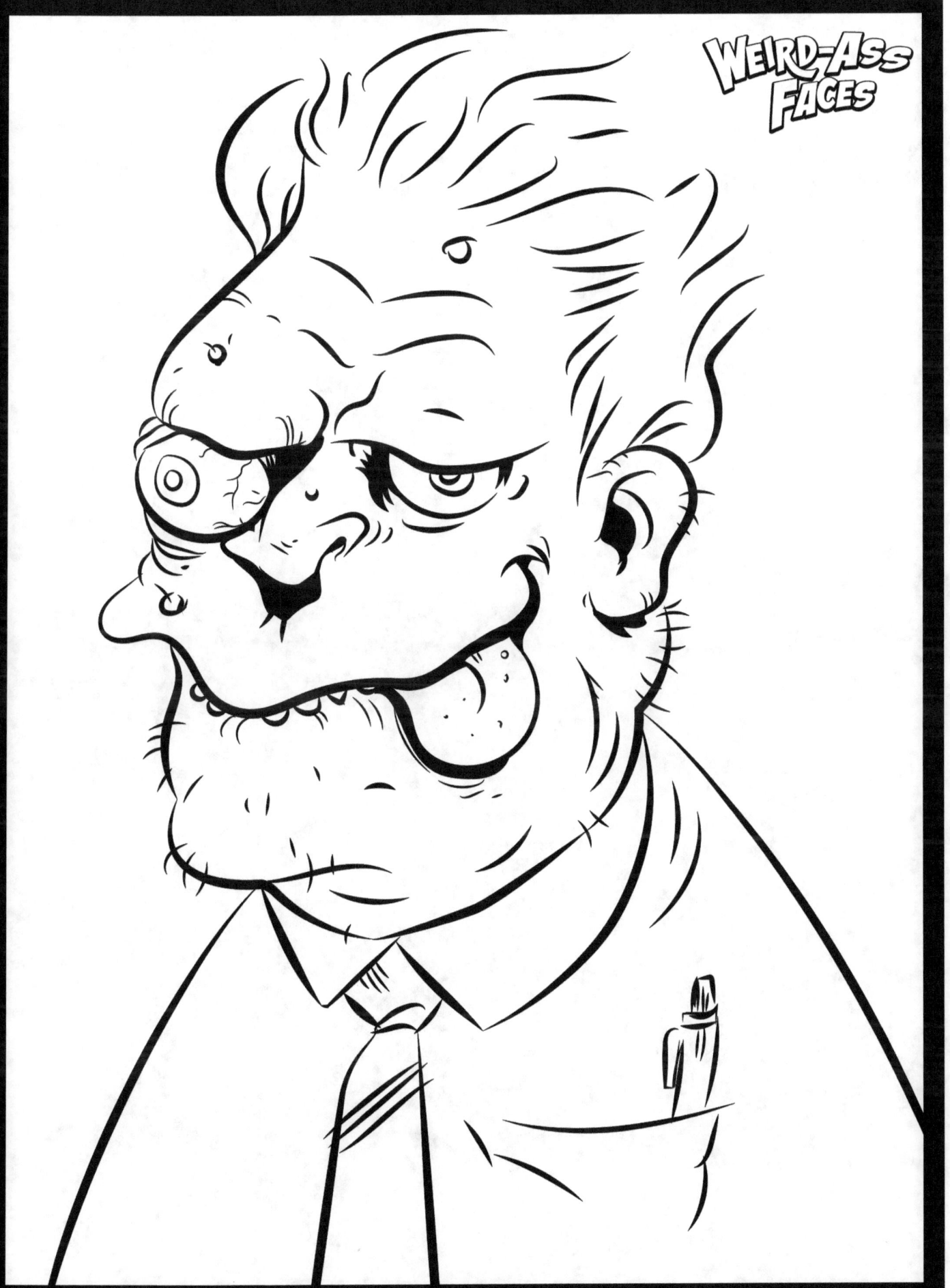

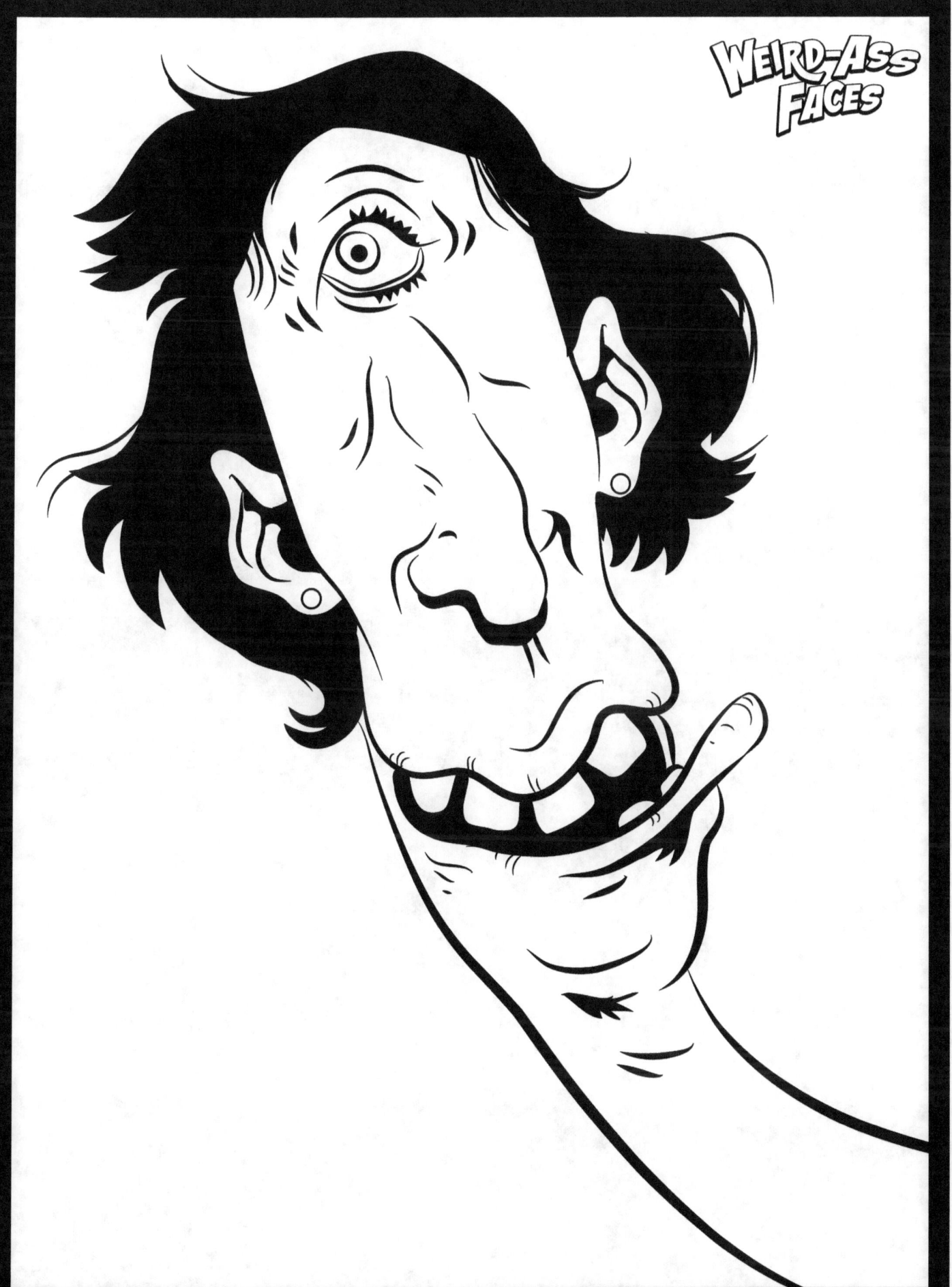

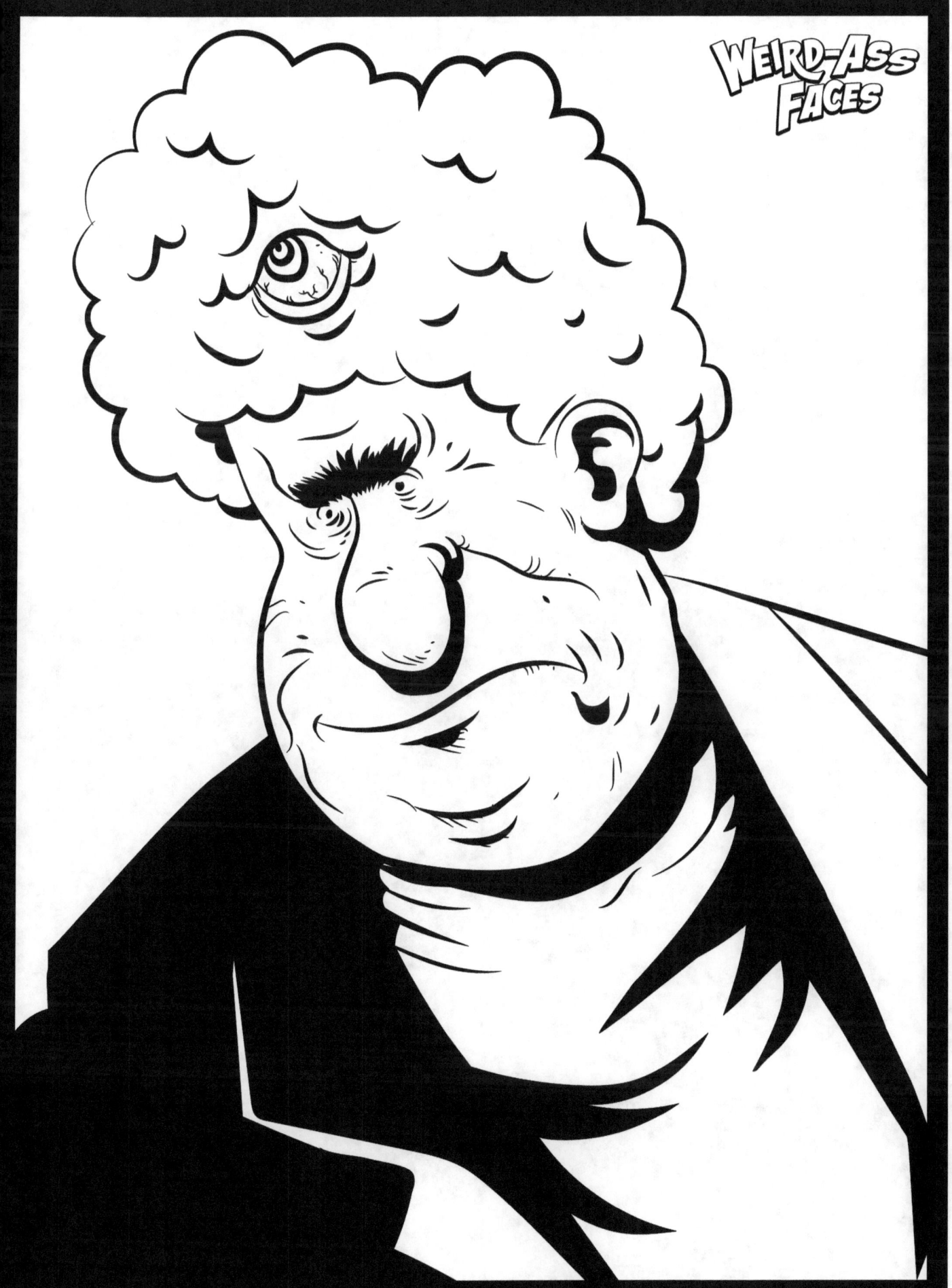

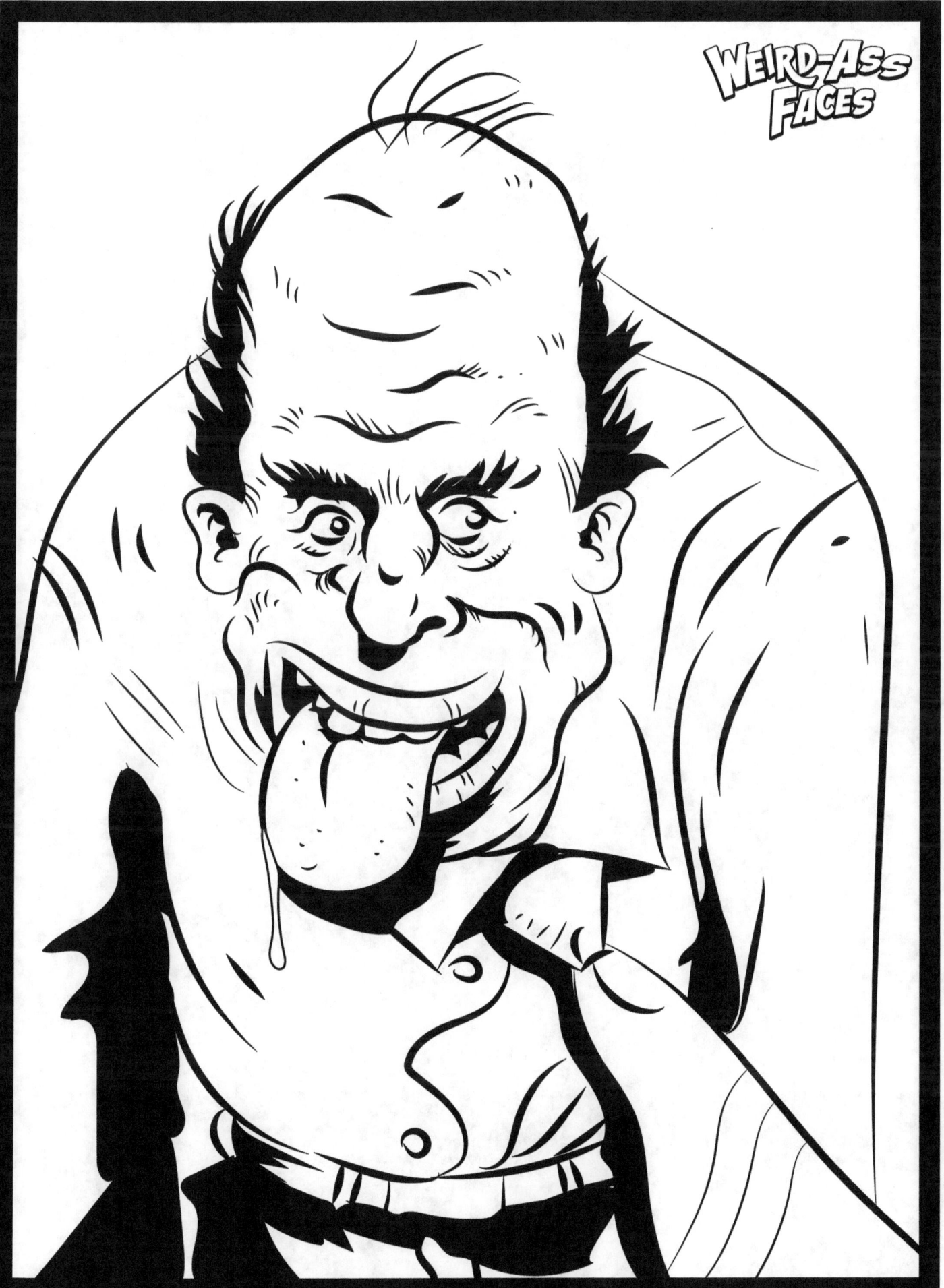

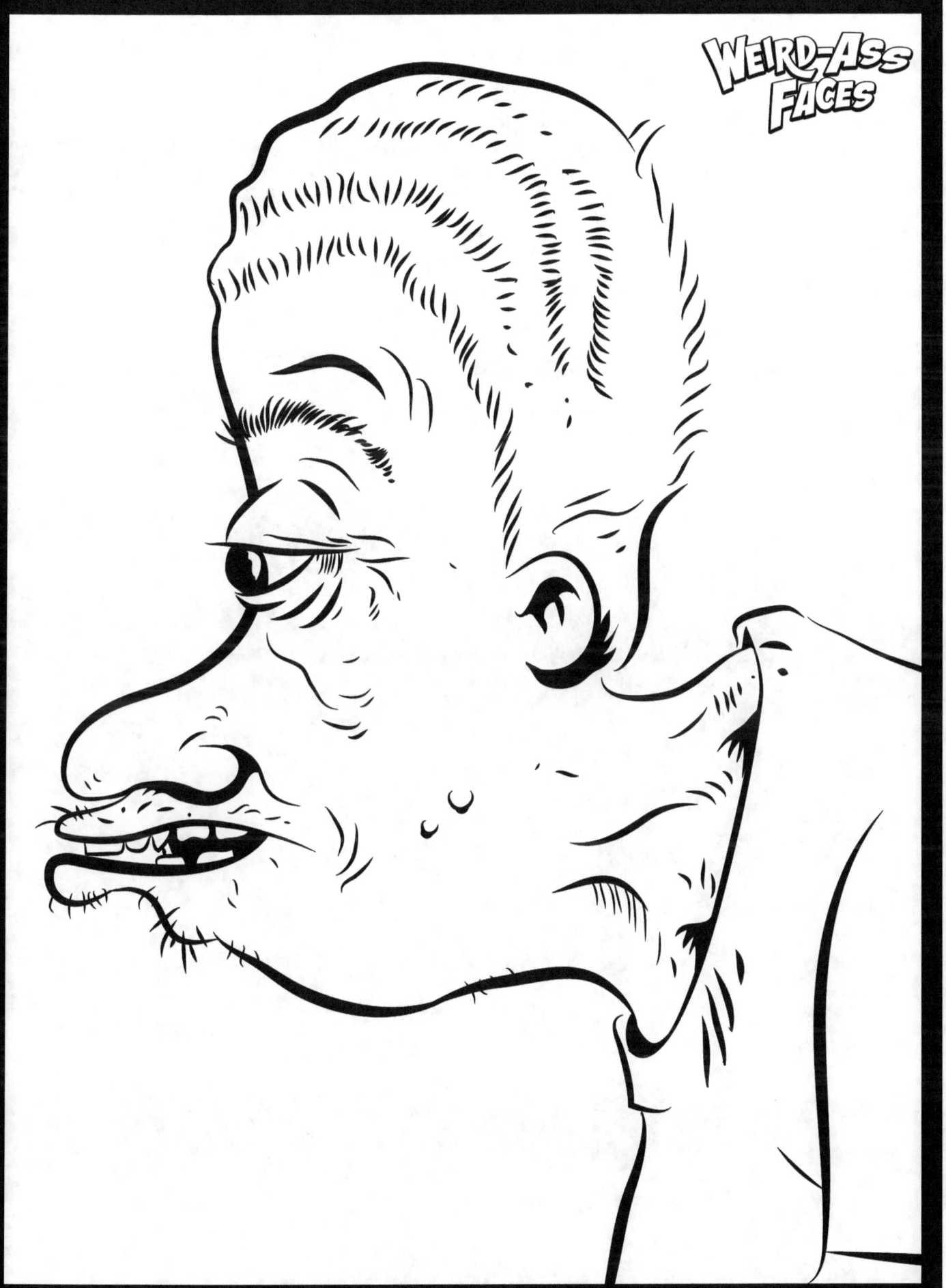

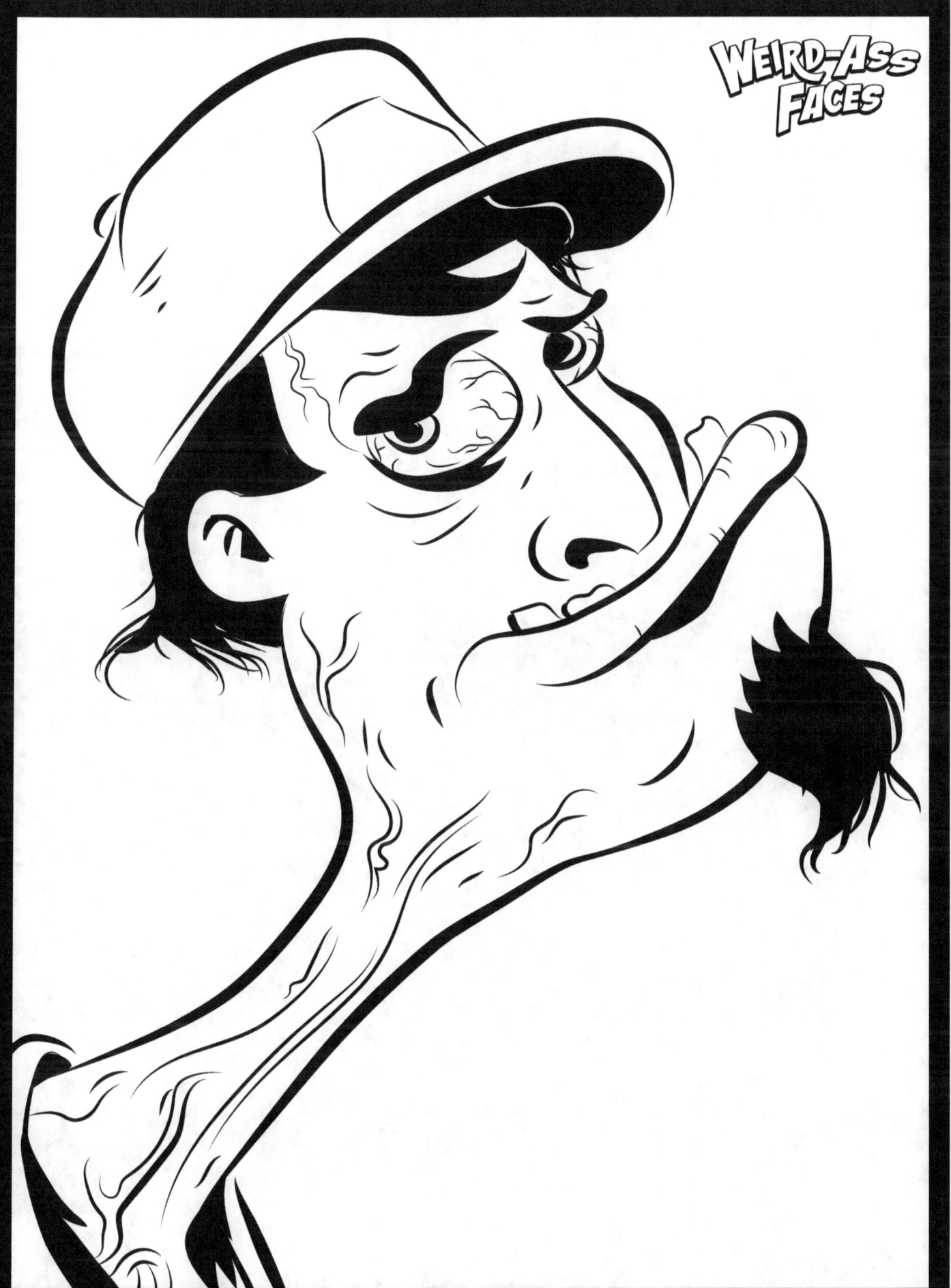

WEIRD-ASS FACES

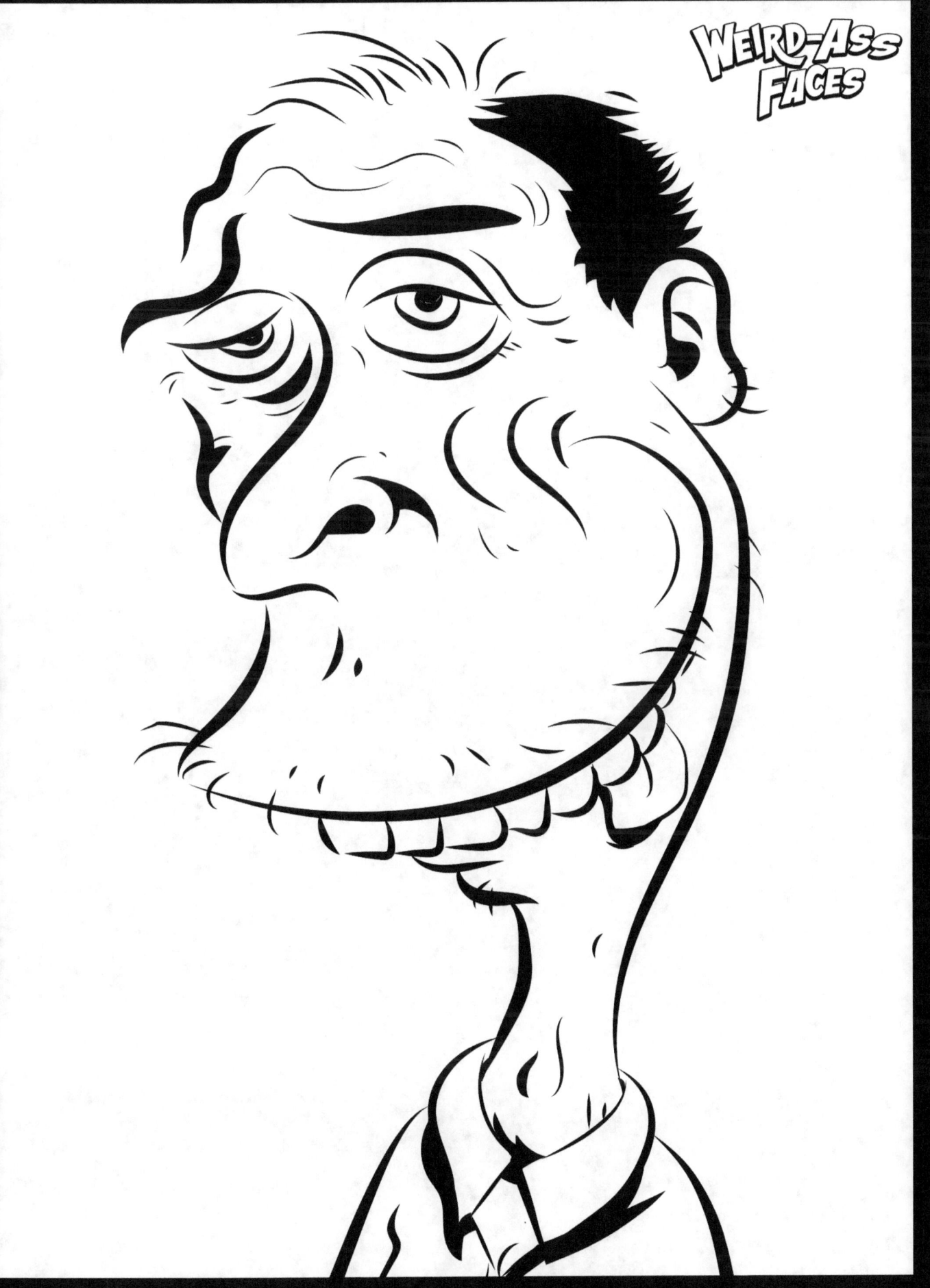

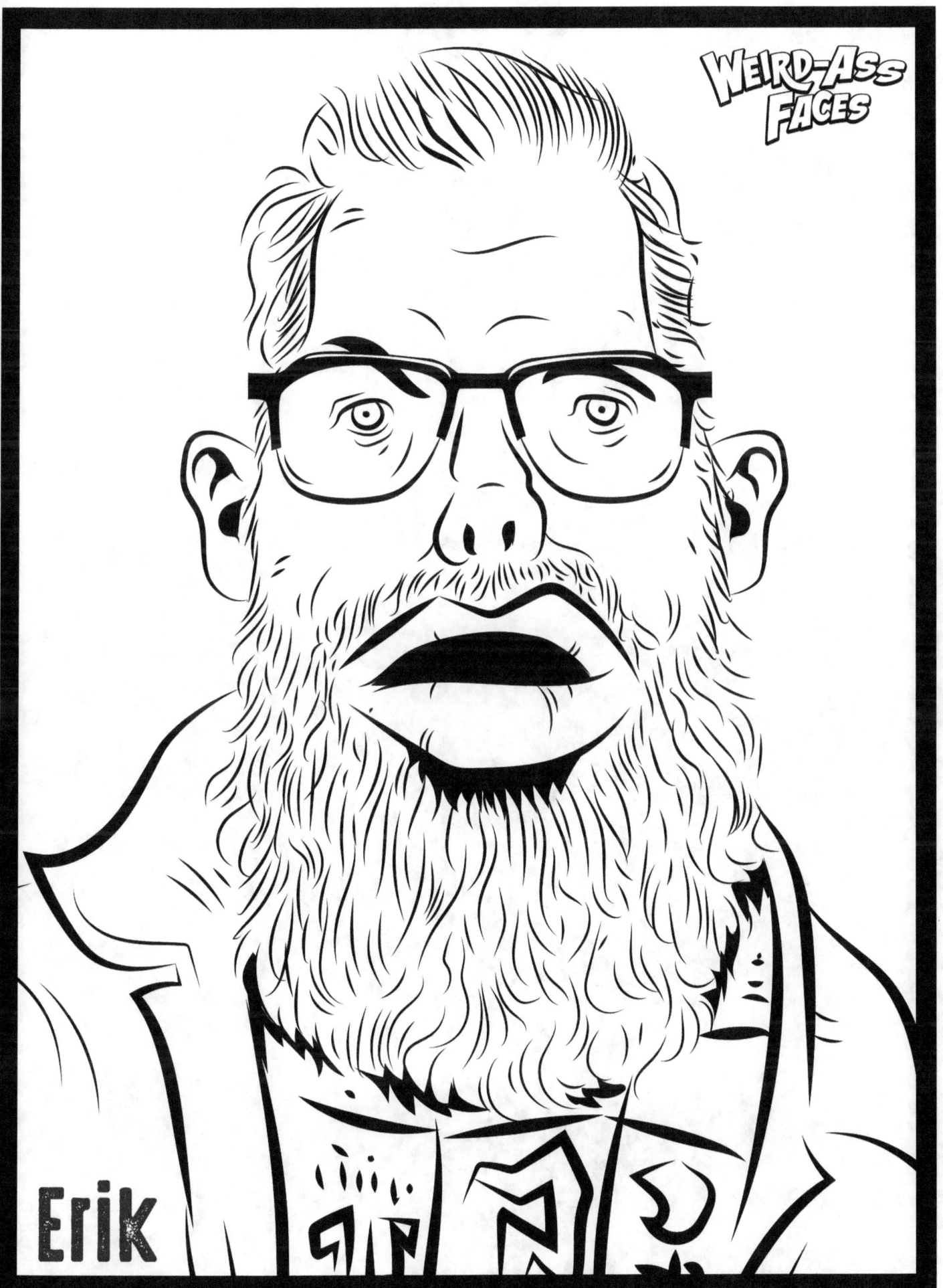

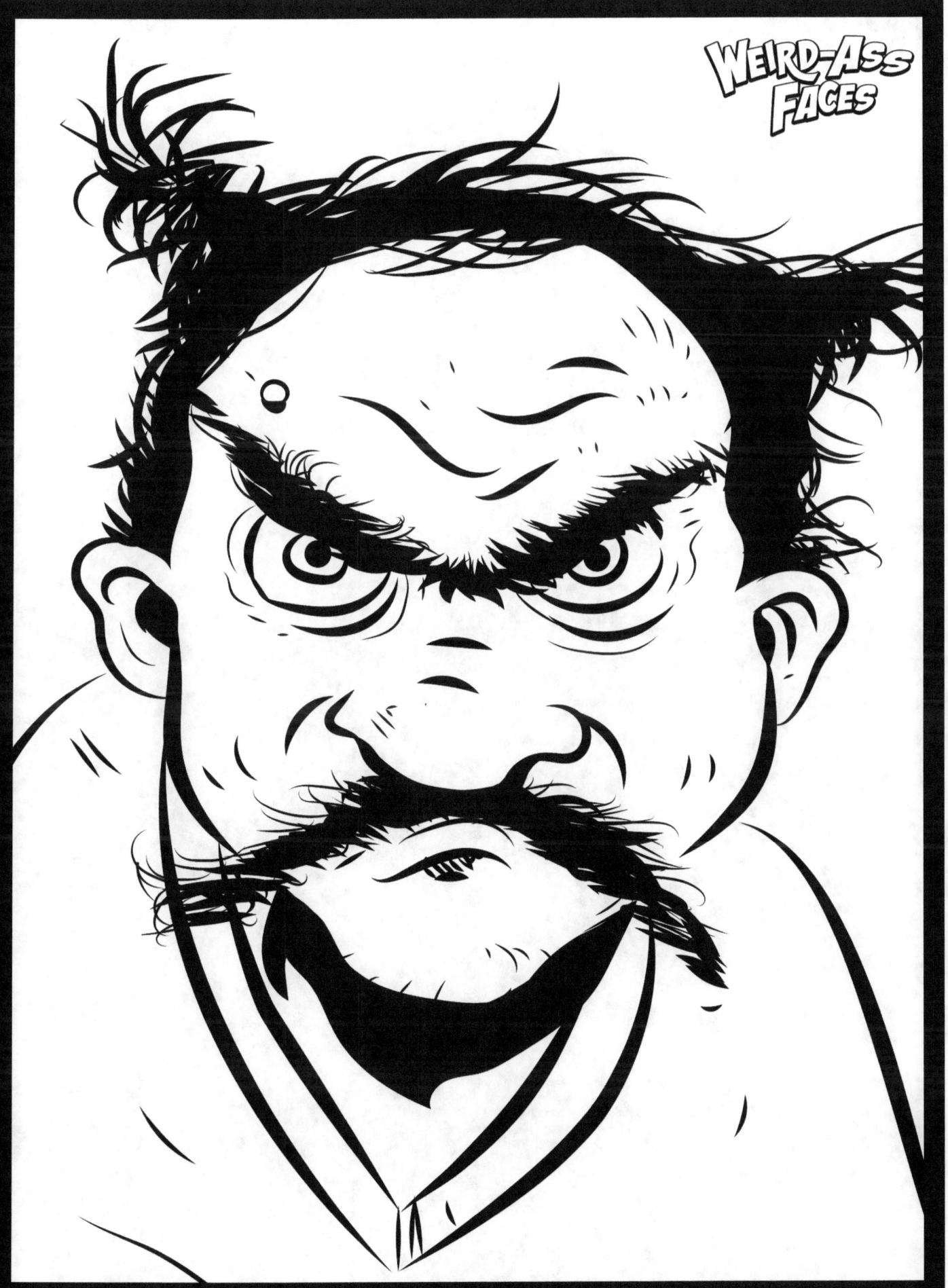

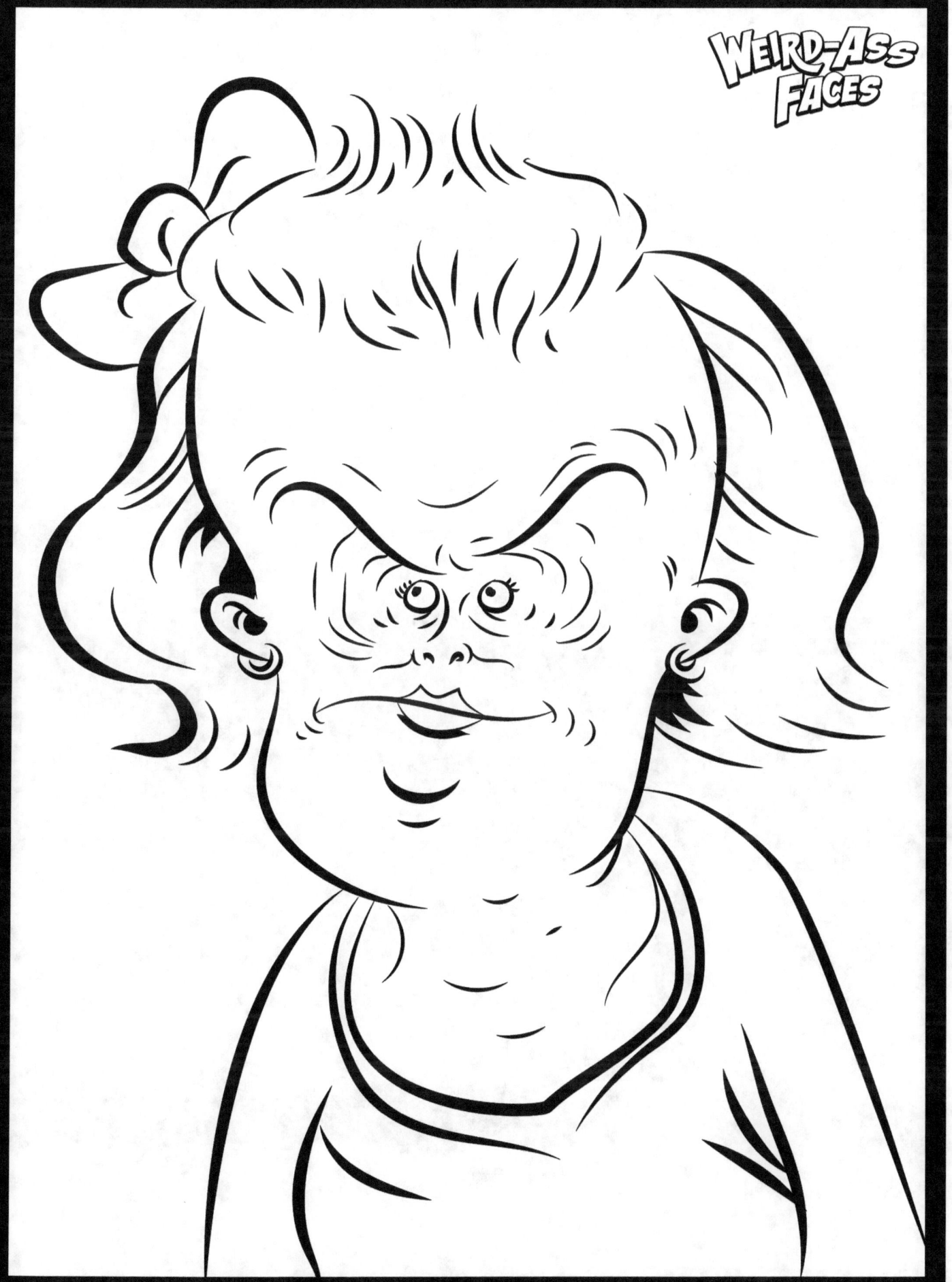

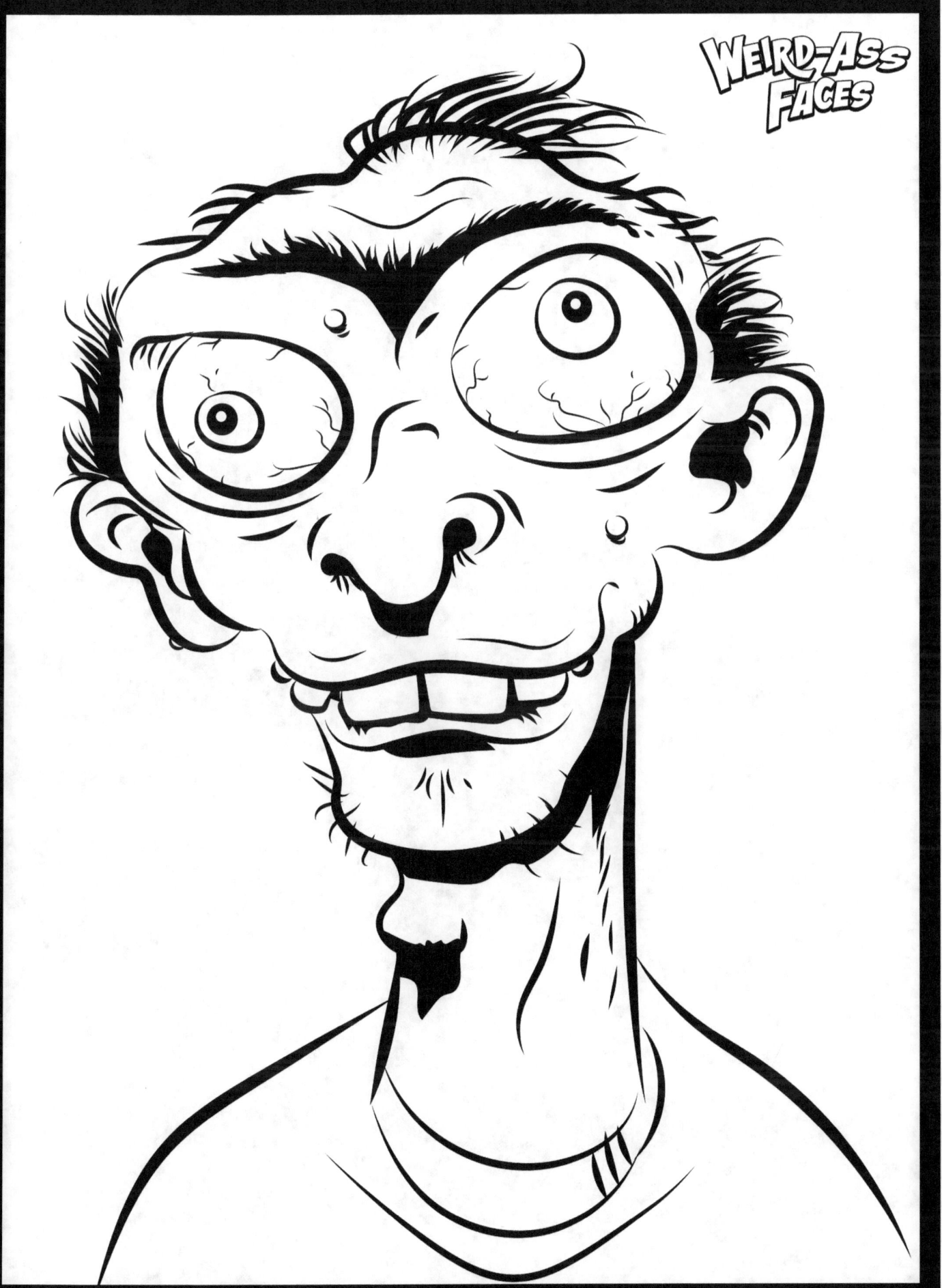

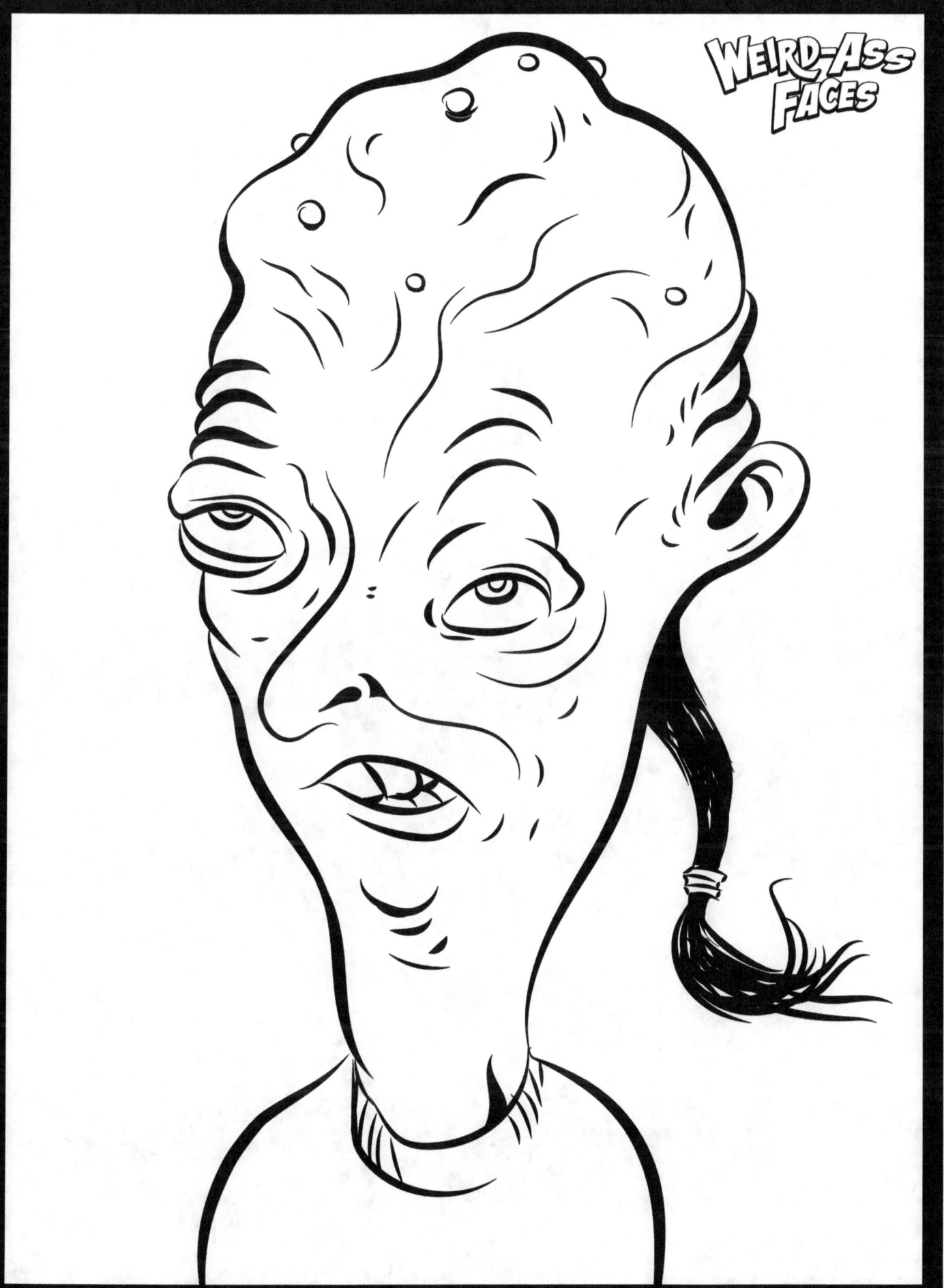

WEIRD-ASS FACES

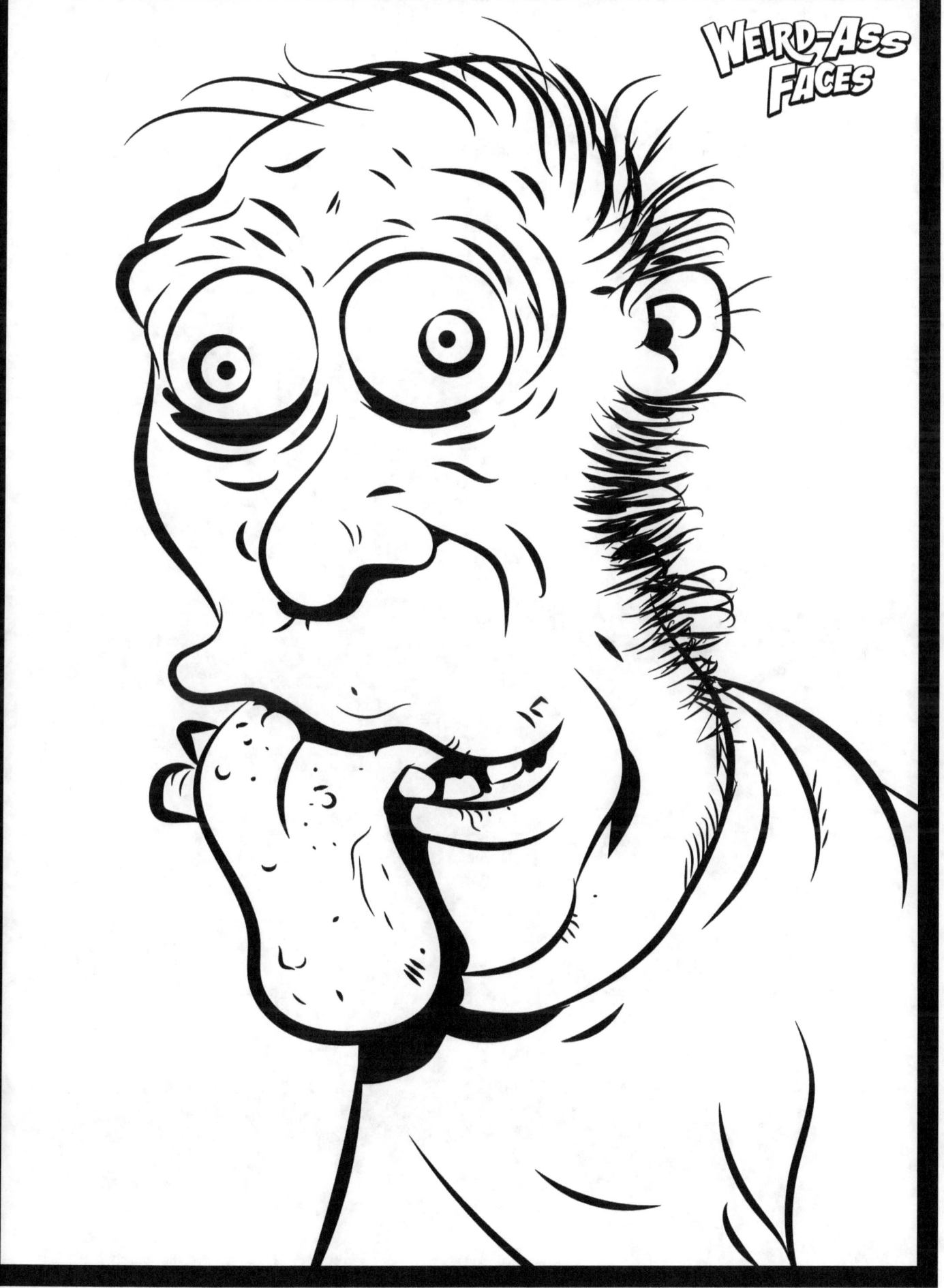

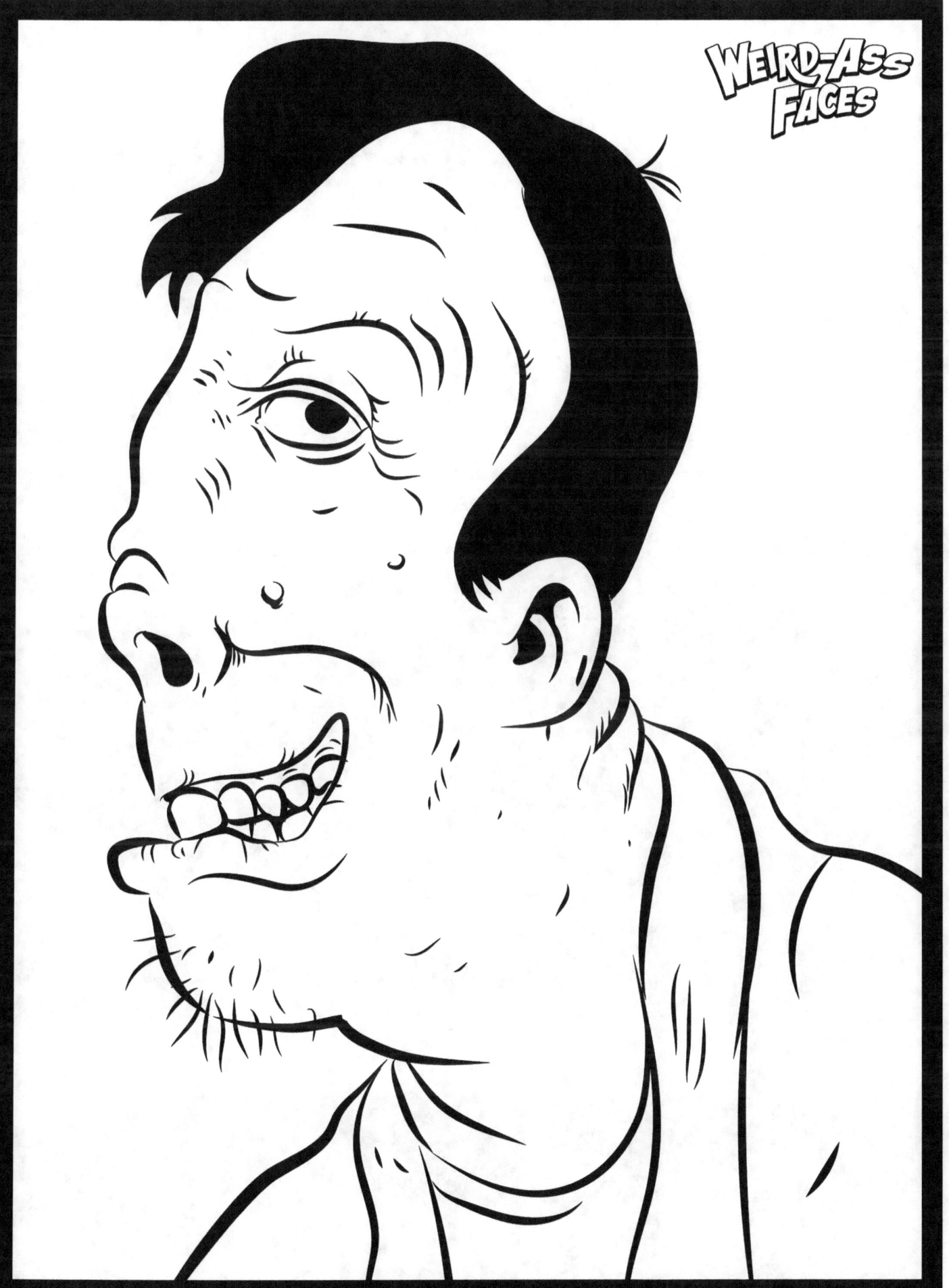

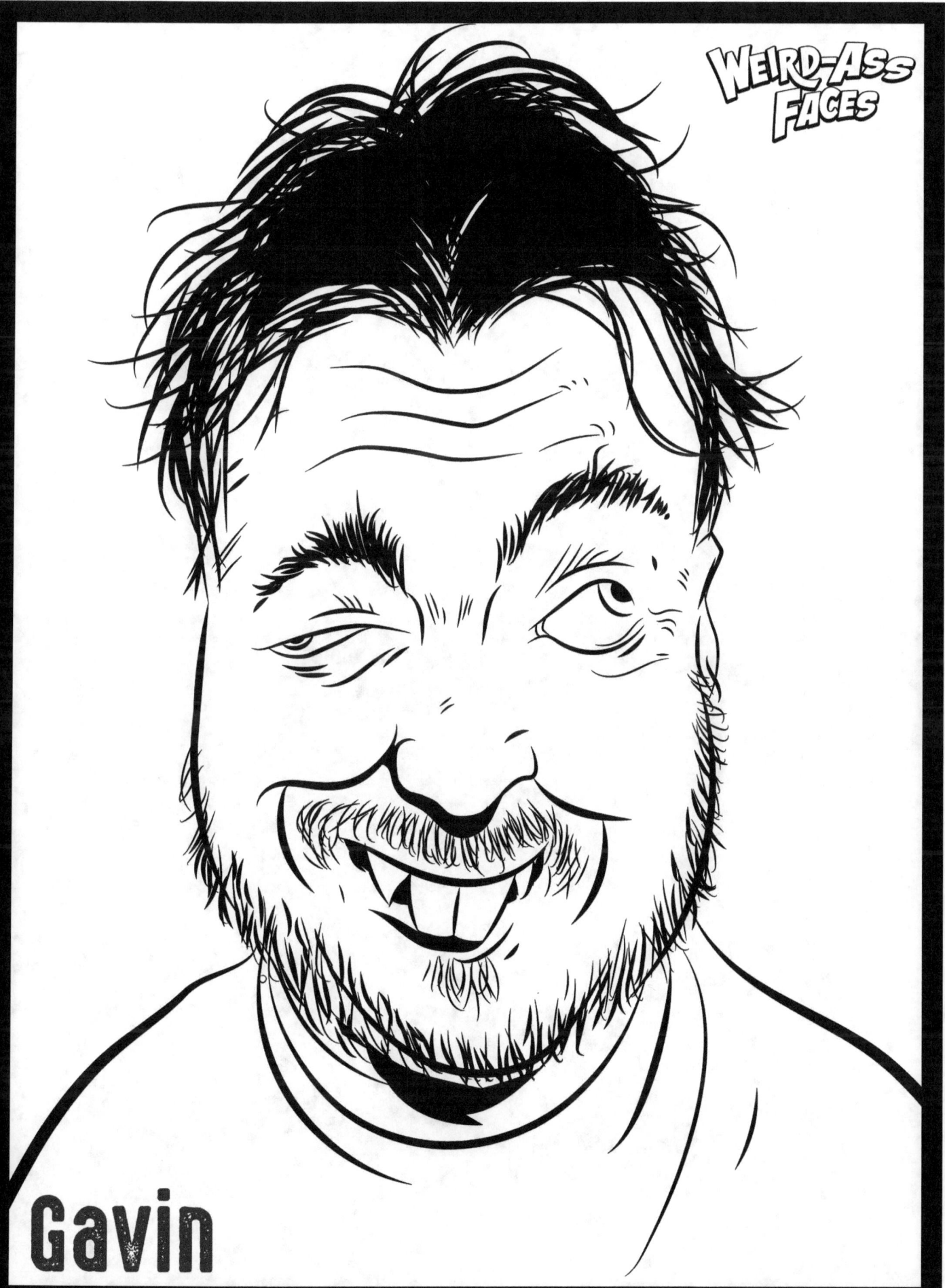

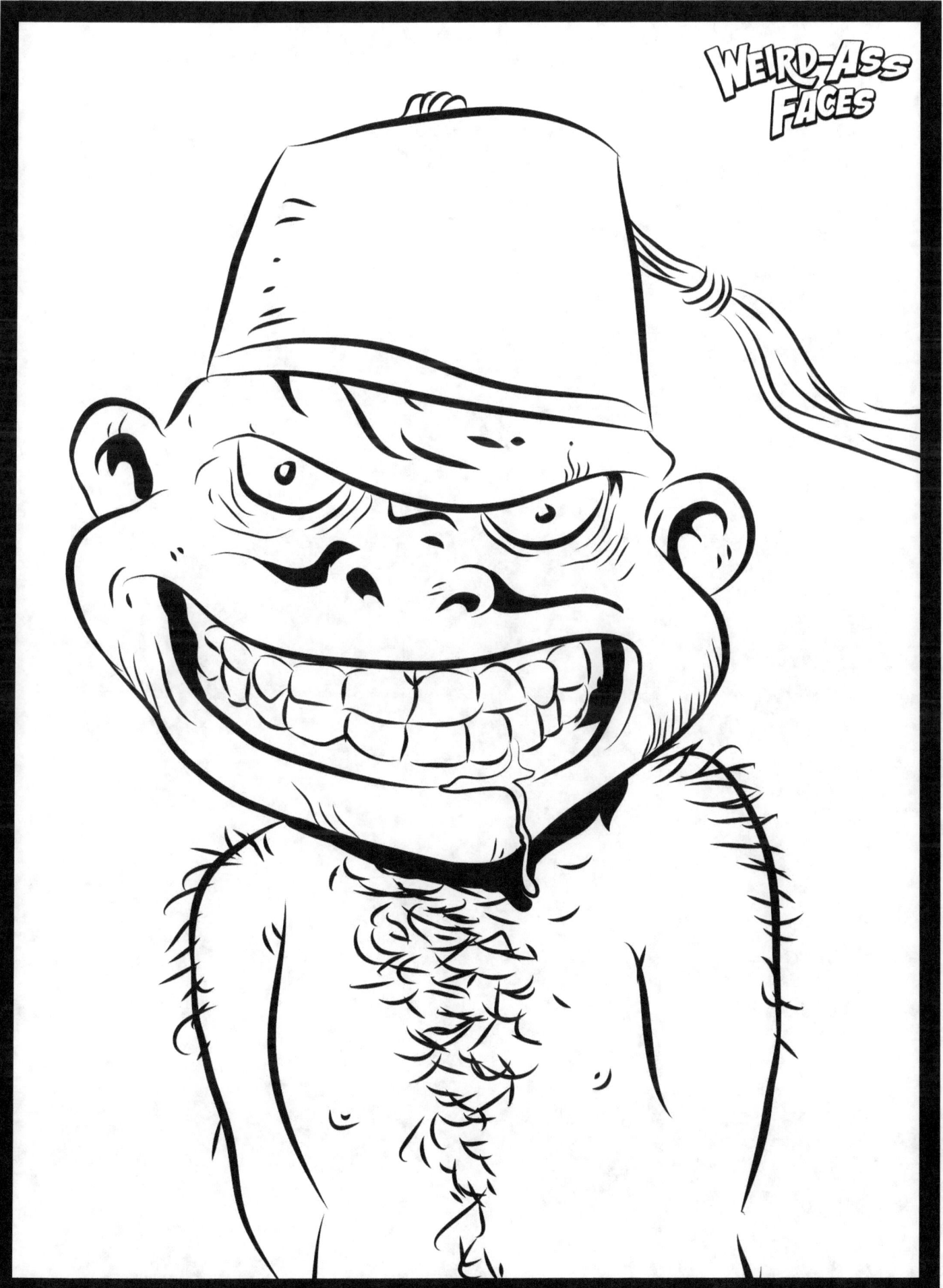

WEIRD-ASS FACES

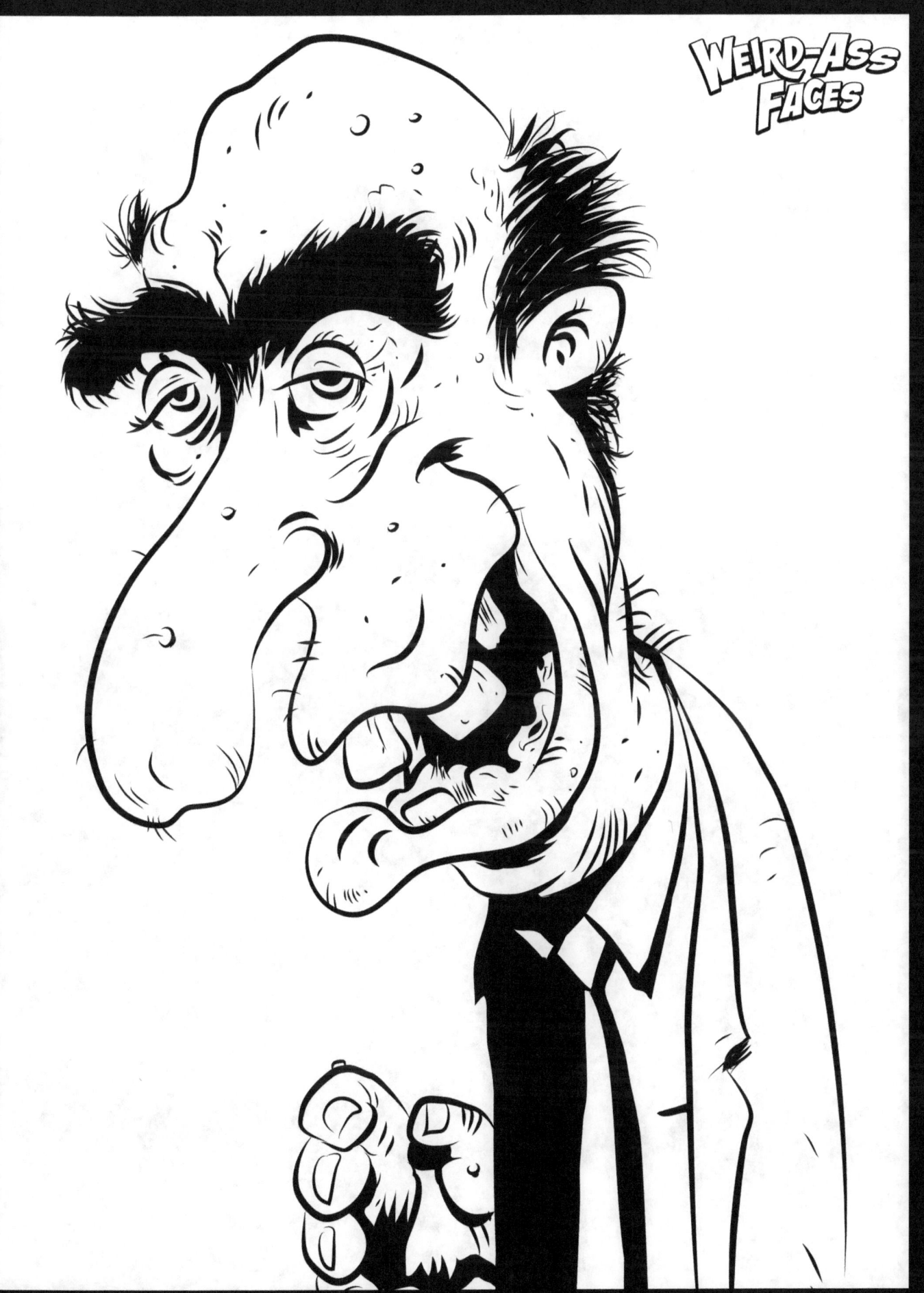

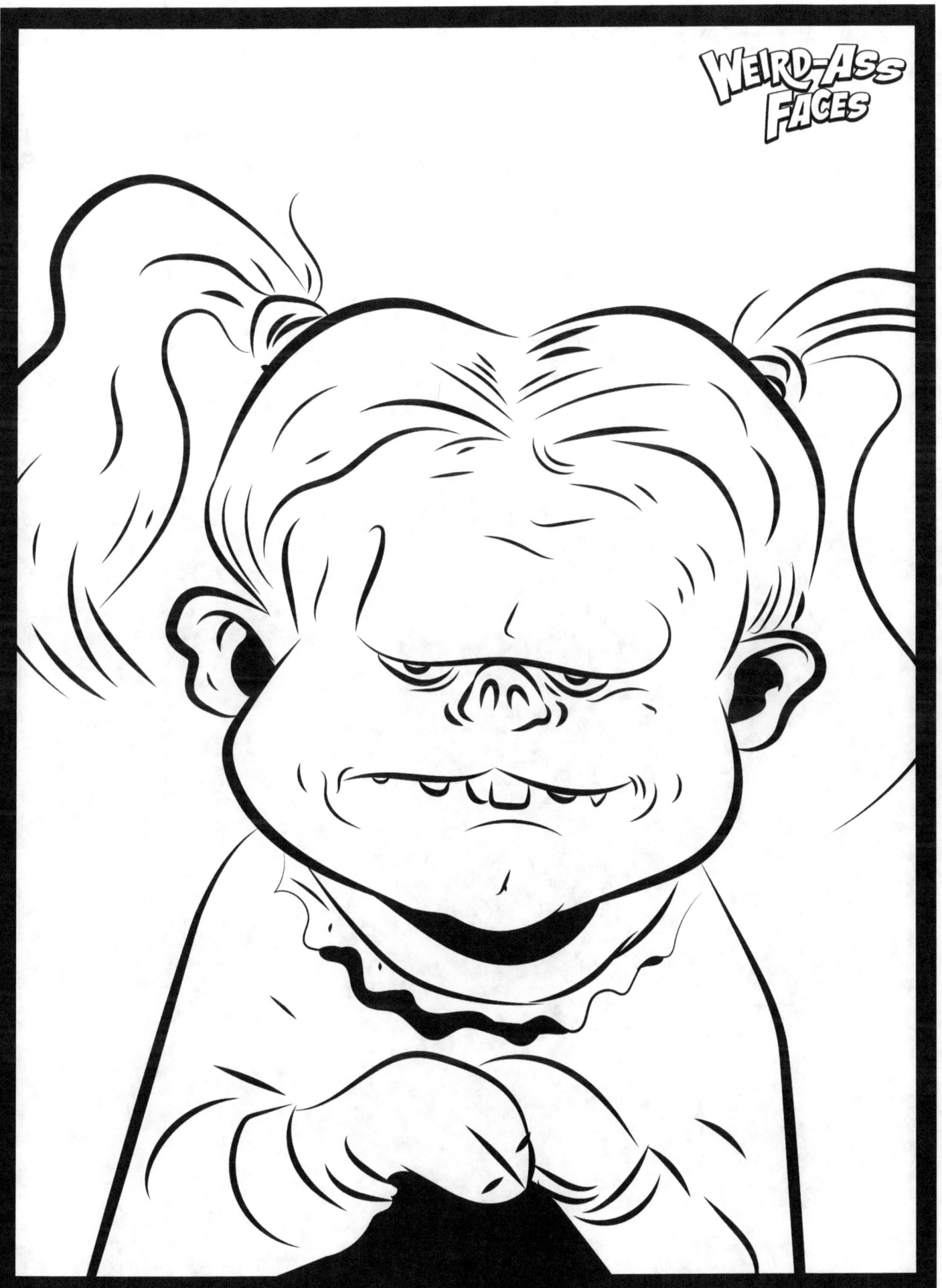

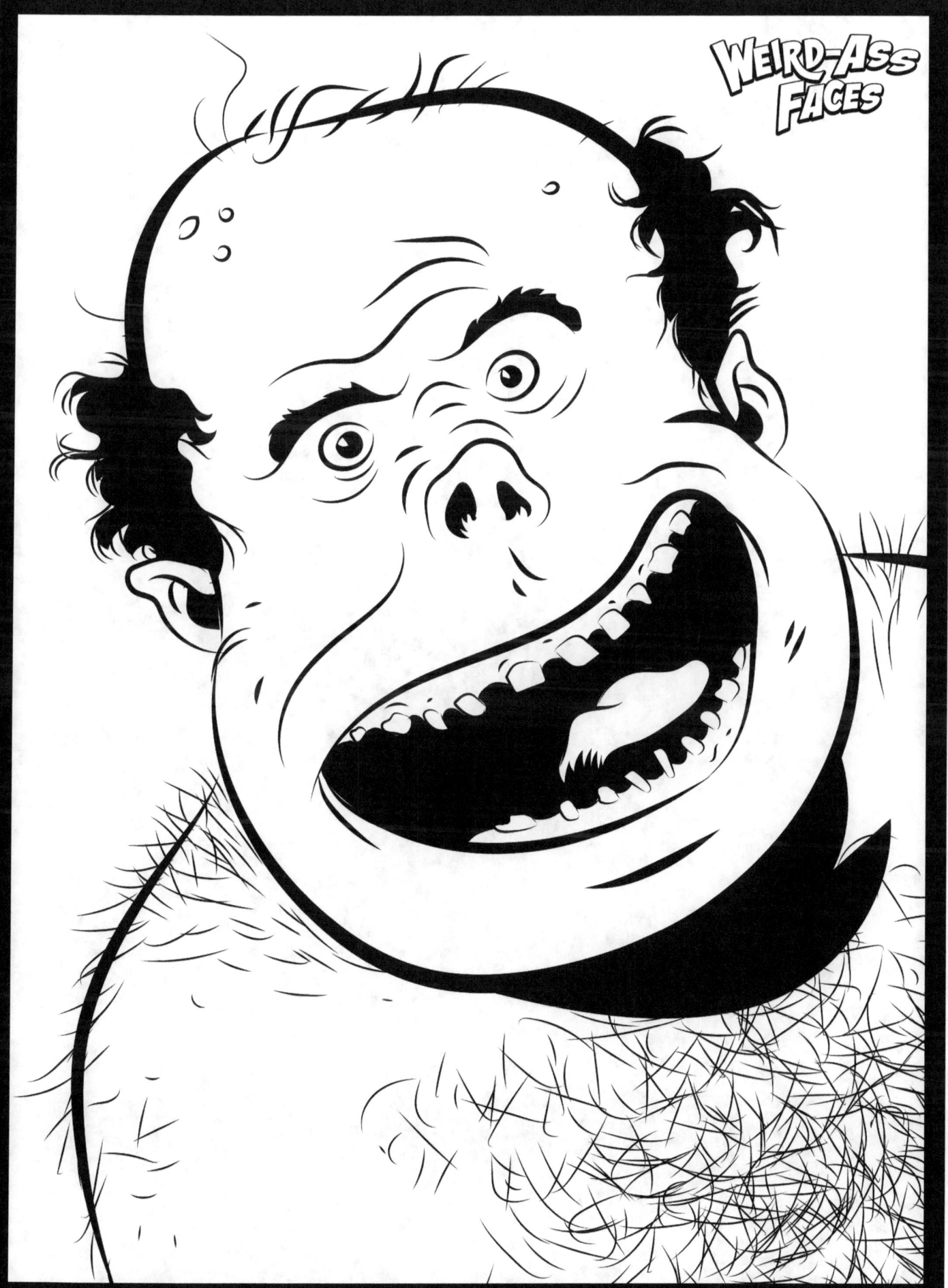

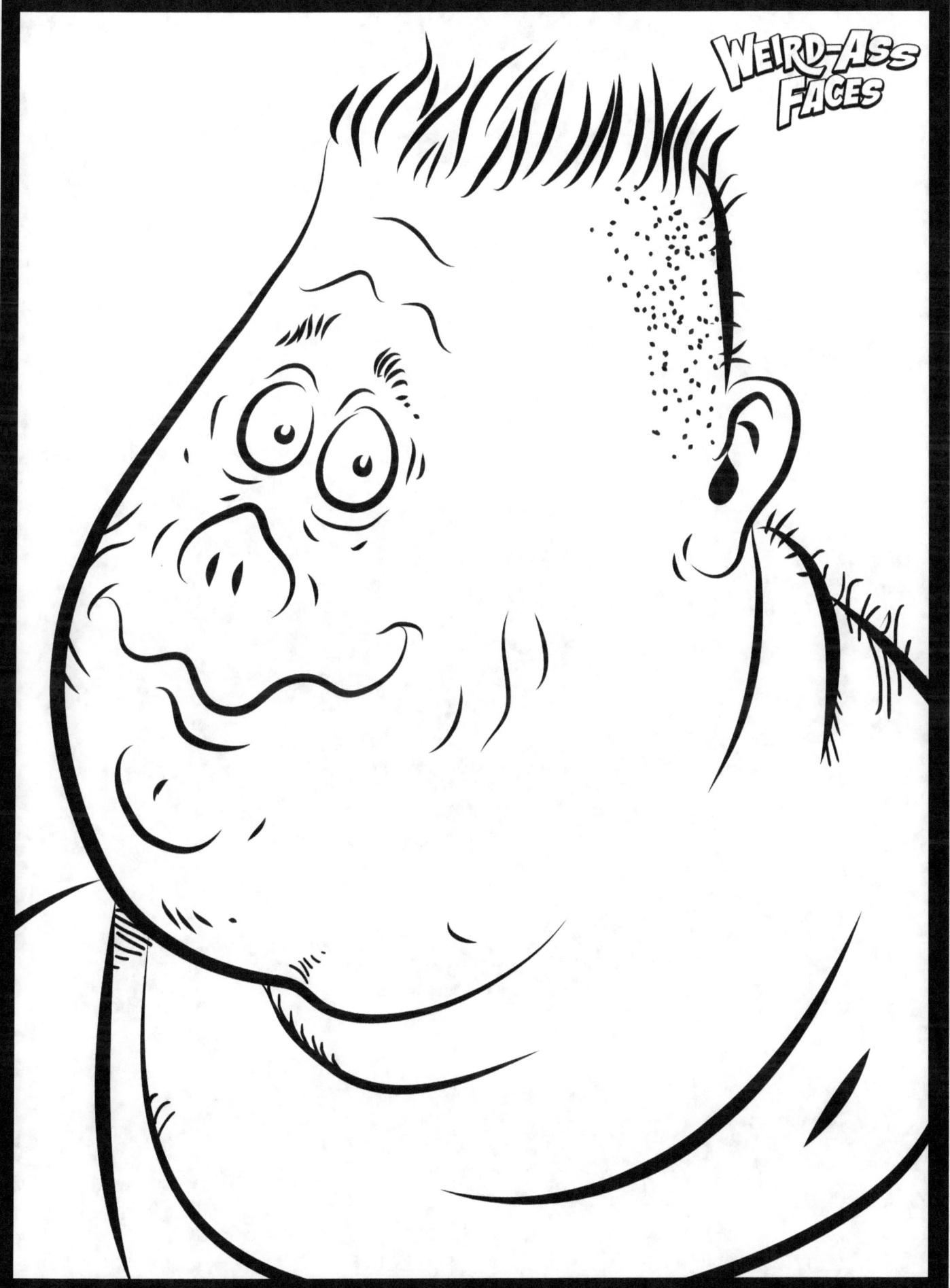

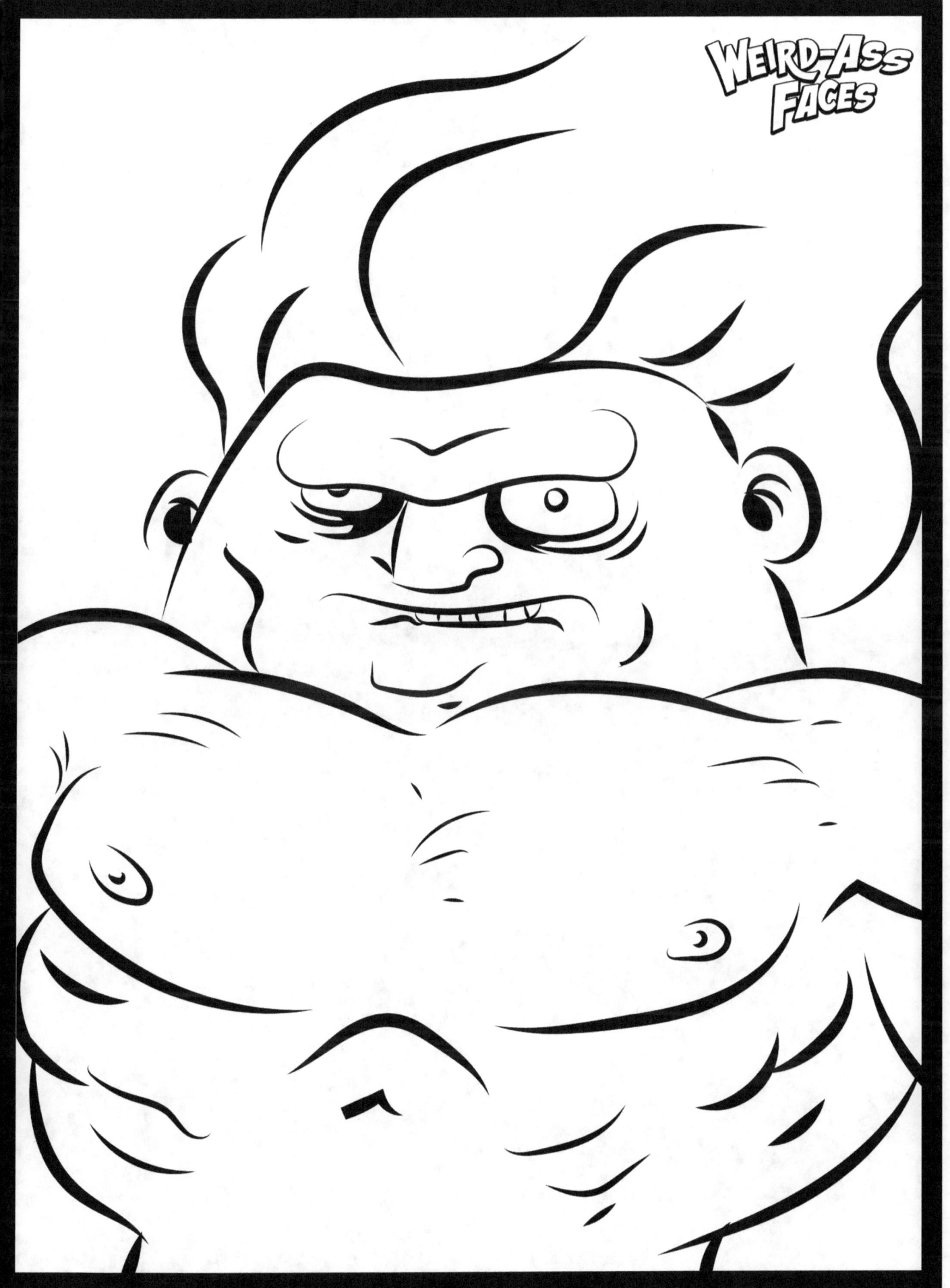

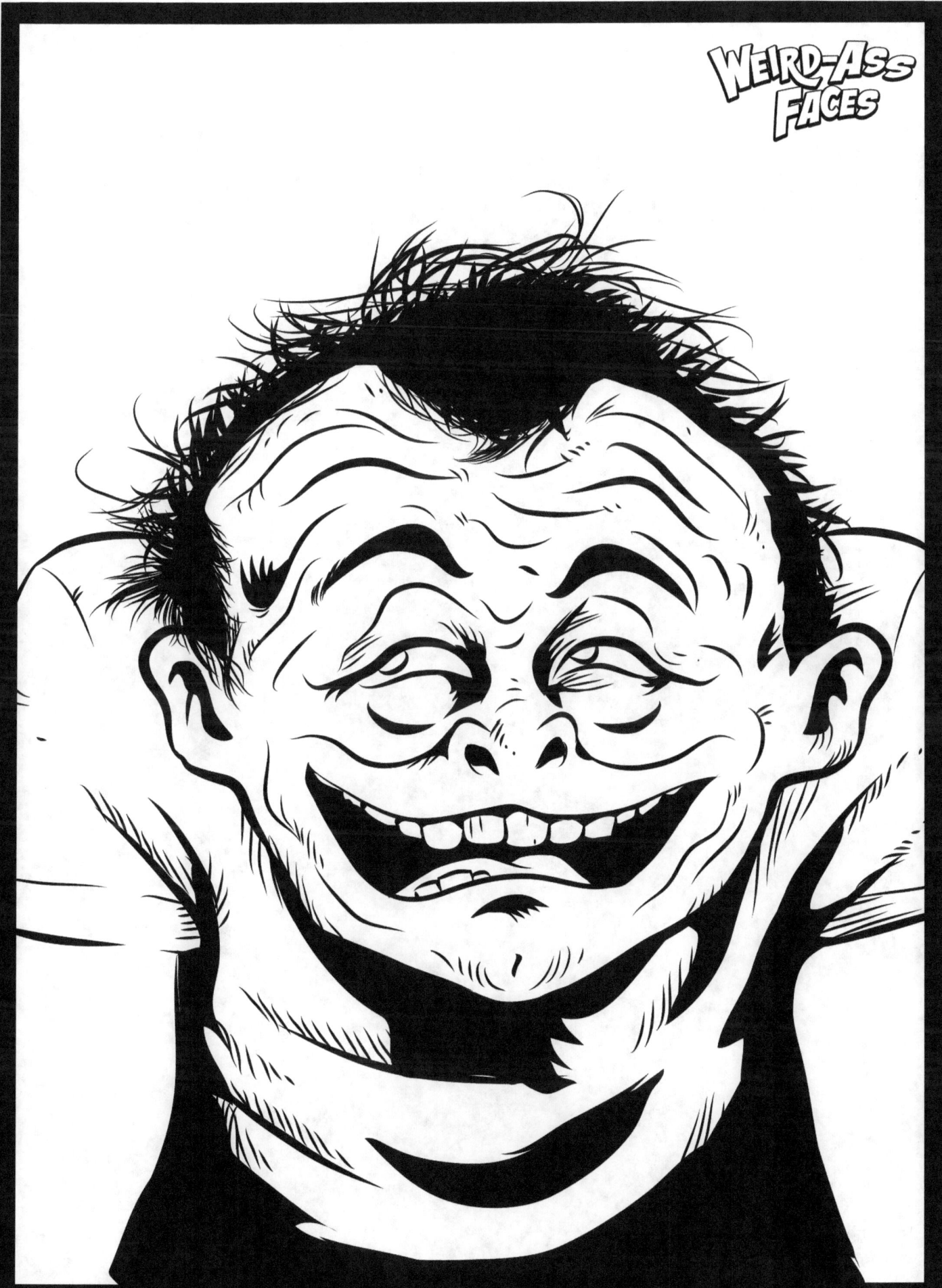

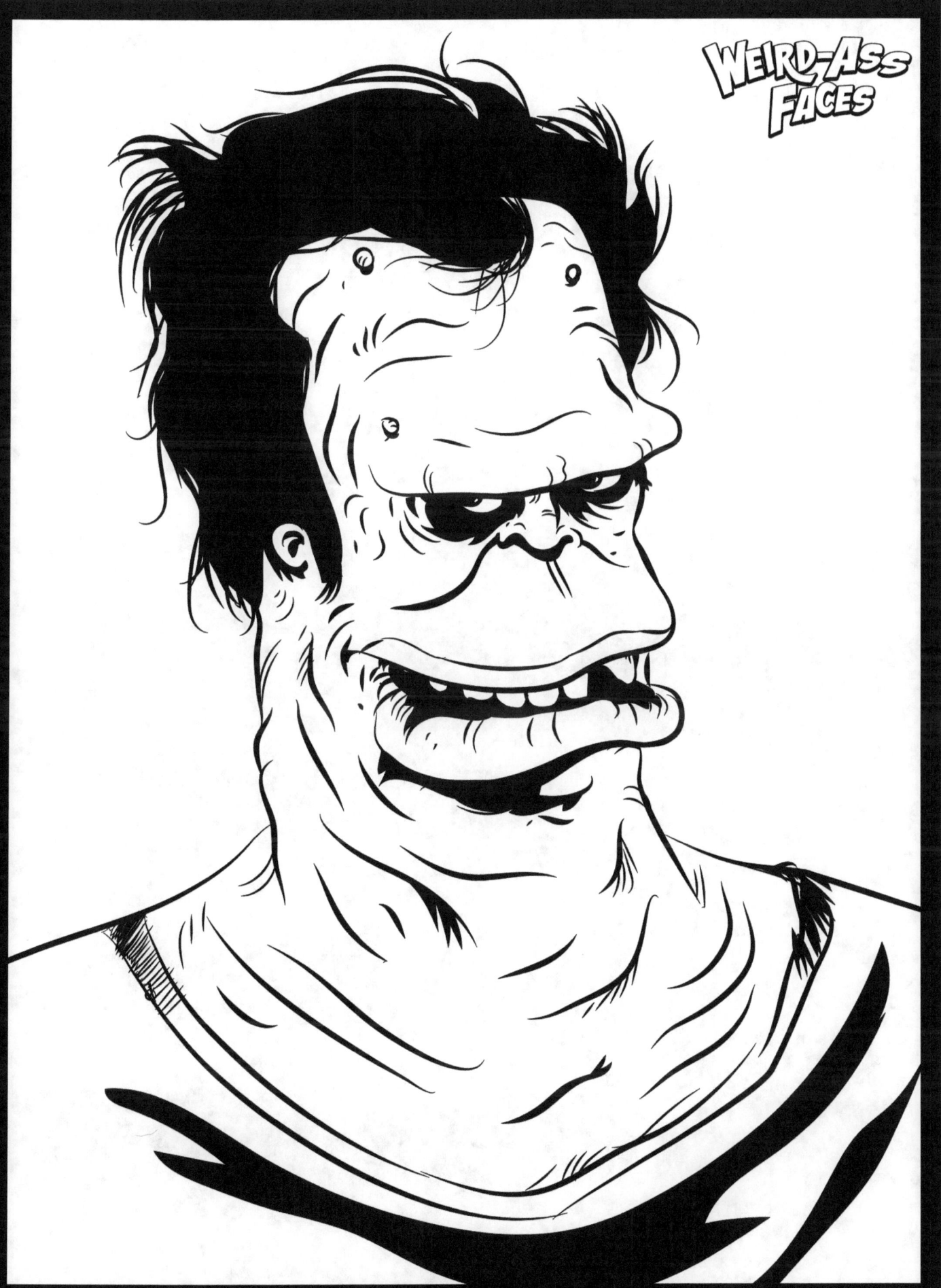

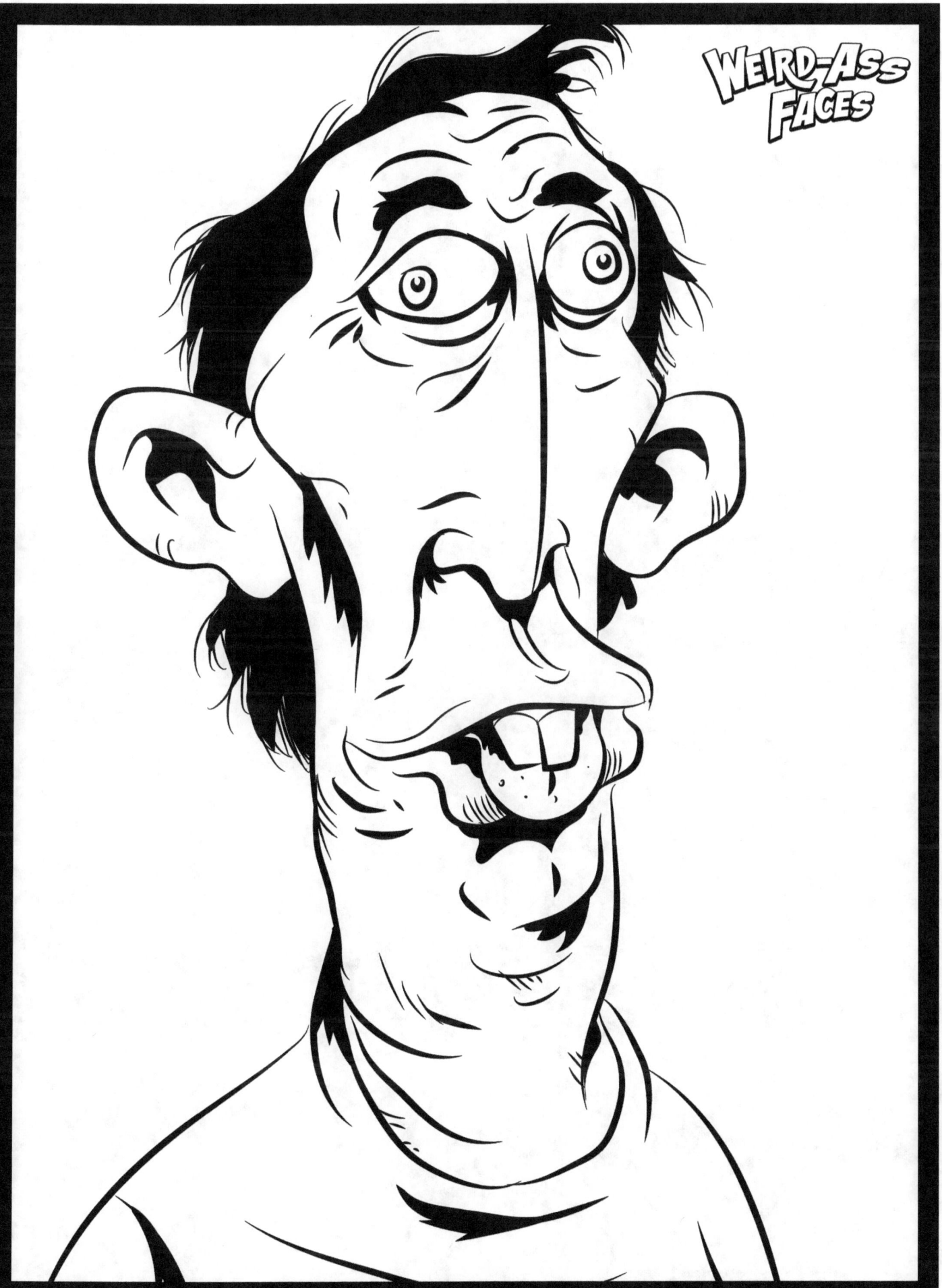

About The Artist

Robert's imagination and desire to draw were first fueled by his frequent visits to the corner newsstand in his Brooklyn neighborhood to purchase comic books, especially those that featured the art of Neal Adams, George Perez, and Jim Aparo. Later, the films seen on local TV, everything from the comedies of Abbott & Costello and The Marx Brothers, B Monster movies and especially the Planet of the Apes series, left a definite imprint in his work. More recently, an interest in Tiki and Pulp Art have been added to the mix. Incorporating an ever-growing cast of Apes, Tikis and appearances from the likes of Doc Savage, Tarzan, The Shadow and more. He is creating a unique narrative through his paintings and sculptures.

Robert's work has appeared on album covers, in publications such as Tiki Magazine and Pinstriping & Kustom Graphics Magazine, and has shown in galleries including Disneyland's Wonderground, Harold Golen, M Modern, Creature Features and Bear & Bird among others. You can also see Robert's work in trading card sets for Topps, Cryptozoic, and Upper Deck on licenses such as Garbage Pail Kids, Wacky Packages, Mars Attacks, Star Wars, DC Comics, Marvel Comics, Ghostbusters, Adventure Time and more. Most notably, Robert worked on 8 paintings for the Upper Deck trading card set FIREFLY The Verse.

Robert is also the author and illustrator of the books:
STRANGEWISE NO.9 and CHIMPS & TIKIS AND RAVEN-HAIRED BEAUTIES: AN ADULT COLORING BOOK.

Find more of Robert's work at zerostreet.com or on Twitter, Instagram, Tumblr and Facebook by searching Zerostreet.

Thanks to my Kickstarter backers! Especially Paolo, Richard, Gavin, Judy and Erik, who all appear in this book!

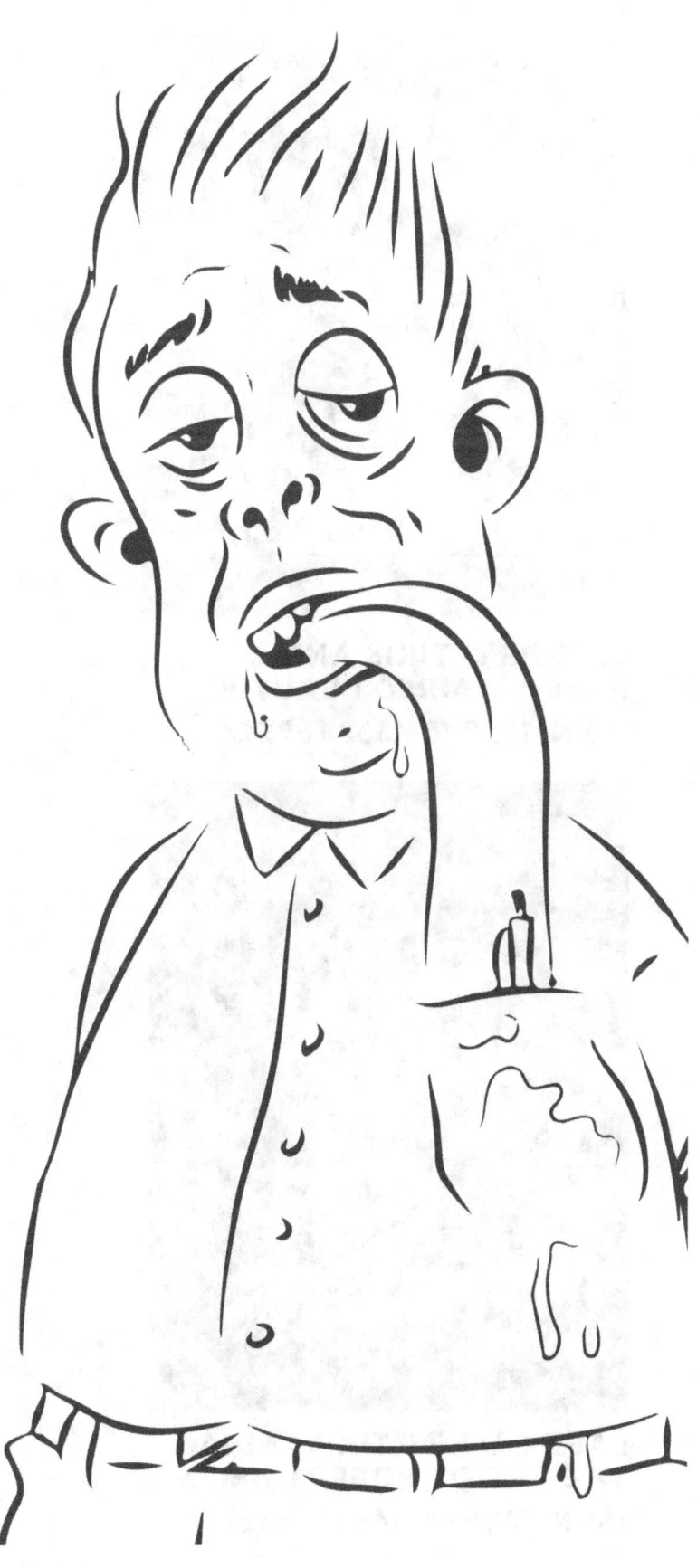

OTHER BOOKS BY ROBERT JIMÉNEZ

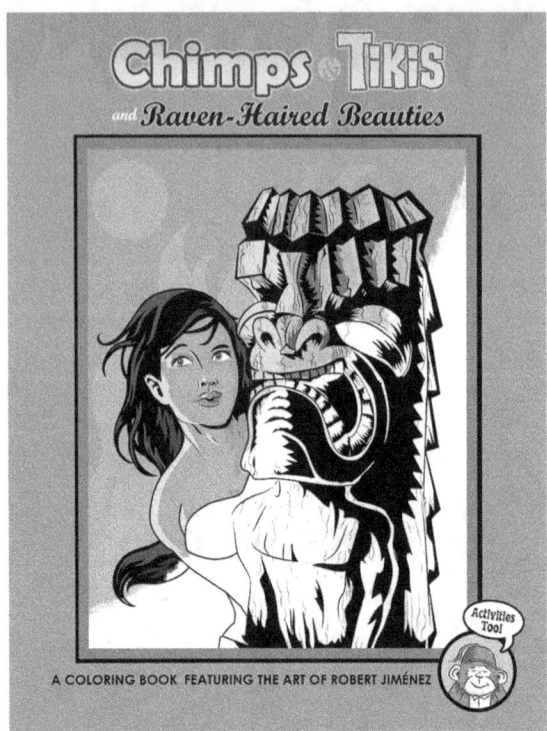

**CHIMPS & TIKIS AND
RAVEN-HAIRED BEAUTIES**
ISBN-13: 978-1533469724

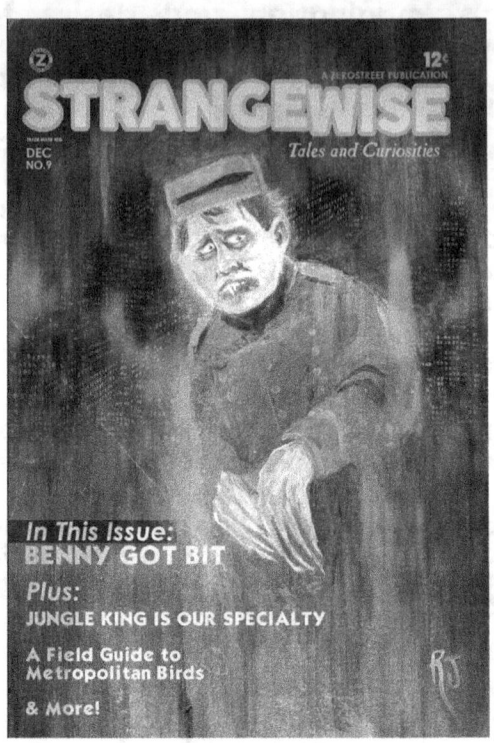

STRANGEWISE NO.9
ISBN-13: 978-1530548408

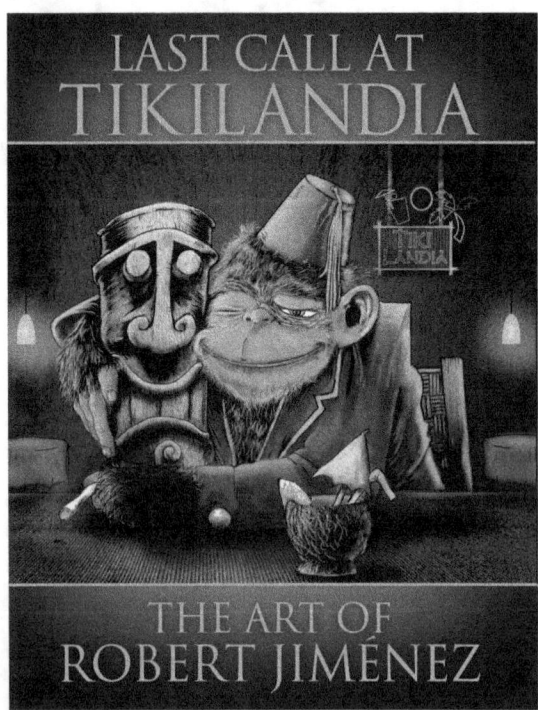

**LAST CALL AT TIKILANDIA
THE ART OF ROBERT JIMÉNEZ**
ISBN-13: 978-1463568627

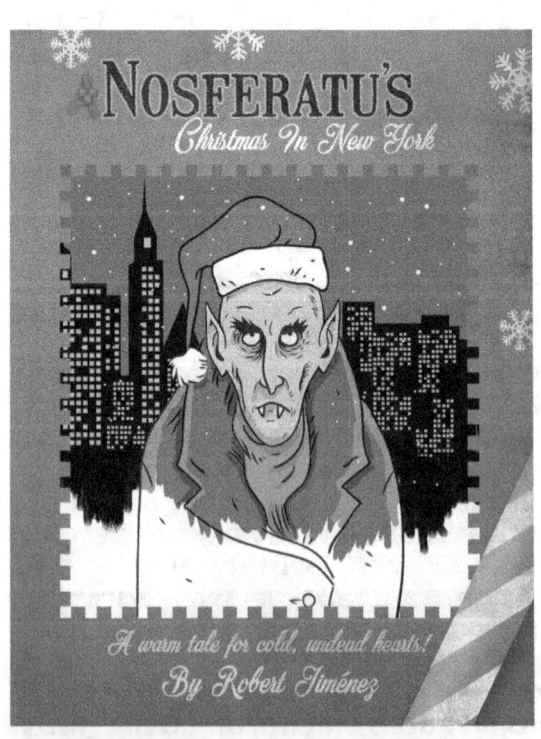

**NOSFERATU'S CHRISTMAS
IN NEW YORK**

ISBN-13: 978-1540334855

www.ingramcontent.com/pod-product-compliance
Lightning Source LLC
Chambersburg PA
CBHW081733170526

45167CB00009B/3804